FORGIVENESS
...It Is NOT
What You Think
It Is!

PHYLIS SPARKS

FORGIVENESS
...IT IS *NOT*
WHAT YOU THINK IT IS!

Learn What It REALLY is!
HOW to do it!
KNOW when you've done it!

BALBOA.
PRESS
A DIVISION OF HAY HOUSE

This book is a work of non-fiction. Unless otherwise noted, the author and the publisher make no explicit guarantees as to the accuracy of the information contained in this book and in some cases, names of people and places have been altered to protect their privacy.

Balboa Press books may be ordered through booksellers or by contacting:

Balboa Press
A Division of Hay House
1663 Liberty Drive
Bloomington, IN 47403
www.balboapress.com
1 (877) 407-4847

The author of this book does not dispense medical advice or prescribe the use of any technique as a form of treatment for physical, emotional, or medical problems without the advice of a physician, either directly or indirectly. The intent of the author is only to offer information of a general nature to help you in your quest for emotional and spiritual well-being. In the event you use any of the information in this book for yourself, which is your constitutional right, the author and the publisher assume no responsibility for your actions.

Print information available on the last page.

ISBN: 978-1-5043-5999-3 (sc)
ISBN: 978-1-5043-6000-5 (hc)
ISBN: 978-1-5043-6025-8 (e)

Library of Congress Control Number: 2016909723

Balboa Press rev. date: 08/02/2016

CONTENTS

Part 2

**Diagnosing and Correcting Problems with
The Soul-Math™ Formula**

Part 3
Turning Things Around

ACKNOWLEDGMENTS

Thank you to everyone in my life who has played a role in the creation of this book by supporting my intention to touch people's lives in a way that guides them into a human experience of peace, happiness, personal strength, and success in actualizing their dreams and desires.

My husband and soul mate, Bill Lange, has been my rock to lean on and the sounding board for guiding me in revealing the marvels and effectiveness of understanding true forgiveness, how to actually do it, and how to know when you've done it. He's my supporter, my source of honest feedback, and the one who offers me warm and loving arms of encouragement.

Thank you to those who have shown up in my life offering me opportunities to forgive in a way that has unfolded a true definition of forgiveness, leading me to discover, develop, and prove a process that actually works to heal the emotional charge of unforgiveness and restore one's peace and happiness.

A special thank you to Christine Imbs, Linda Keck, Dr. Mackenzie McNamara, Chris Bryant, Rev. Polly Lemire, and many others who helped, encouraged, and nudged me to complete this book.

INTRODUCTION

The words *I forgive you* can be three of the easiest words to say and mean, or the most difficult. For instance, let's say that after you've had a really tough day at work your spouse forgets to pick up the dry cleaning, even after being reminded. No big deal, right? But let's say your beloved forgets your tenth wedding anniversary. That's a little tougher, but getting over it is still doable. But what if you find out that this person is having an affair? Okay, now you've got a problem.

Of course, it's nothing new to say that forgiveness is important. The value of forgiveness has been touted as an act of virtue and a mandatory command in every philosophy and religion including Christianity, Judaism, Islam, Hinduism, and Buddhism. Its importance has long been recognized by every branch of the medical profession, especially psychology and psychiatry, as vital to our health.

Still, for most of us, the act of forgiveness is not that simple. Even if threatened with Divine retribution or the possibility of a stress-related illness, forgiving someone who has deeply hurt us is hard. In fact, those of us who claim to have forgiven someone in all likelihood really haven't, and it's hurting us more deeply than we consciously realize or can even imagine. And what if we subconsciously, or even consciously, hold on to self-blame, shame, or guilt, replaying the past in our present moments; moments that should be devoted to living life in peace and happiness? Self-forgiveness can be one of the hardest things to do.

So exactly what does it mean to *truly* forgive, how do you actually do it, and how do you know if you've *really* done it? You might even ask yourself, "Do I really *have to*? I mean, I didn't cause the problem, did I?" These are valid questions that we'll dig into in the coming pages. More importantly, I'll share with you the Forgiveness Process that I discovered and developed while going through my own painful struggle with fear, anger, torment, and unforgiveness. I have shared this method with many people over the years who now realize how *authentic* forgiveness can change their lives, and that *it wasn't what they thought it was!* A good example is the following testimony from Jonathan, who used the Forgiveness Process along with The Soul-Math Formula, also included in this book:

> The Forgiveness Process is doing wonders in my life. As intense as it is, it is liberating in that it is setting me free to be true to myself in areas of my life that I probably never have been before. I have now lost 35 pounds, am looking for a new wardrobe, and am meeting new people who are helping me continue the journey. I am learning a new skill, have a new hobby, and am overcoming fear. It is a gradual movement forward in my life from nightfall to morning, and I am cherishing it. I have also been working The Soul-Math Formula, getting in tune with my feelings, thoughts, and beliefs, and how these factors affect the outcome. I am well on my way to a brand new life.

Perhaps Jonathan's example can be an inspiration to you, but it may tempt you to jump ahead to the Forgiveness Process and skip the sections of this book that lead up to it. But please don't do that. It's important to pave the way so when you get to the Process, you'll see forgiveness with new eyes and be even more prepared to initiate the steps.

The accomplishment of authentic forgiveness can make an enormous difference in your freedom to move forward with courage, command, and commitment, leaving all the stumbling blocks behind you. You'll be amazed at the discoveries you make about the obstructions you might have been tripping over as you pursued your dreams. Why not make it easy instead of hard, a journey of thriving rather than striving? Why not unfold a depth of confidence that makes your light shine in ways you never imagined?

Okay, if you're ready and willing, read on. Your new life is awaiting you.

PART 1

EXPLORING AUTHENTIC FORGIVENESS

As long as you don't forgive, who and whatever it is will occupy a rent-free space in your mind.

—Isabelle Holland

CHAPTER 1

ATTEMPTS TO DEFINE "FORGIVENESS"

To forgive is to set a prisoner free and discover that the prisoner was you.
—Lewis B. Smedes

AS CHILDREN, WE were more than likely told that forgiving others was the right thing to do. If we didn't hear it in Sunday school, we heard somewhere, "To err is human, to forgive divine," "Forgiveness is a virtue," "Let bygones be bygones," "Turn the other cheek," and "Forgive and forget." Somebody was always trying to convince us that forgiving another person was the honorable, good, and morally correct thing to do. Many times, along with that instruction came the direct or implied threat of supernatural punishment if we didn't forgive, along with an accumulation of guilt for having held onto a grudge.

Forgiveness has been defined as a voluntary act on the part of a victim to change their attitude toward their offender by releasing and letting go of negative emotions regarding an offense. It has been described as a commitment to giving up grudges, anger, resentment, bitterness, and other hurtful emotional wounds and obstructions to one's peace of mind. Forgiveness has also been described as wiping the slate clean, canceling a debt, or pardoning someone who has wronged you. Now I'm not suggesting that such definitions are wrong, but they are superficial and fail to pierce the depths of one's subconscious storehouse of false beliefs that may be causing hesitation, limitation, procrastination, stagnation, and general unhappiness. These buried beliefs foster low self-worth, blame, resentment, and other deeply submerged agitations, and can only be faced and forgiven when revealed at a conscious level.

There are all kinds of suggestions floating around on how to forgive, including seeing things from the other person's point of view or realizing by holding onto negative reactions we do nothing more than hurt ourselves. These suggestions may soften the intensity of blame and anger, but the results are often short-lived. Very seldom do they have a lasting effect upon the reasoning mind of the victim who seeks justice, revenge, or, at the very least, an apology from the offender.

As a result of some bullying aimed at me when I was a child, I remember my mother trying to comfort me by teaching me to chant back, "Sticks and stones may break my bones, but words will never hurt me!" Later in life, I realized that this had done nothing but fling my anger back at the person who flung their nastiness at me. It may have made me feel a bit stronger, and temporarily pulled me out of my own self-pity, but in reality all it did was add to the debris of unresolved anger in my subconscious mind. I carried this unconscious emotional burden throughout my life. That is until I consciously recognized it for what it was and learned how to truly forgive and free myself.

There are many superficial directives floating around for handling hurt, anger, victimhood, and various other emotional pain. These suggestions or instructions often include the act of forgiveness. But the sad fact is, what most people perceive as forgiveness is simply an "out of sight, out of mind" approach in an effort to make themselves feel better. They then become blind to what's stored in the subconscious mind, weighing them down and burdening them like a heavy, toxic emotional backpack. This invisible backpack often grows over time and impedes their progress toward a life of fulfillment and success. Very few have grasped the fact that unforgiveness lurking in the mind and heart eventually takes a toll on one's physical and mental health and well-being, as well as the joy of living.

The one thing most everyone seems to agree on is that forgiveness opens the way for greater health, happiness, and freedom to move on with one's life. But what is it, *really*? How do you *actually do it*? And how do you *know* for sure that it's been done? Oh, it could be a matter of simply *letting go*, but what in the world does that mean?

Before I offer my viewpoint on what forgiveness *really* is, I think it's important to clarify what **unforgiveness** is so that you know what you're dealing with as you apply the Forgiveness Process.

What Is Unforgiveness?

The answer to this question seems obvious. Most everyone would say that unforgiveness is the opposite of forgiveness.

Well, to expand upon the obvious, unforgiveness is the emotional replay of past events in the present moment every time someone or something triggers a memory of those events. Unforgiveness is about being frozen or stuck in a mental and emotional reaction to a perceived wrong aimed in your direction. Once you react with hurt feelings, self-pity, feelings of abandonment, resentment, bitterness, anger, hatred, or revenge, and then continue to indulge in these feelings when reminded of the memory, *that* is unforgiveness.

For many, unforgiveness is an "eye for an eye" mentality, a burning desire to get back at the perpetrator and the insistence that the culprit pay for what he or she did.

Unforgiveness can also apply to one's attitude toward one's self. A person may be anchored or emotionally stuck in the goo of self-blame, shame, or guilt, with no lasting remedy for truly forgiving him- or herself and enjoying the freedom of self-respect and self-acceptance.

Most people simply do not understand how damaging unforgiveness can be to their mind, body, and spirit. Emotional resentment can fester and grow, poisoning your spirit and burdening your soul. These debilitating and toxic feelings create blocks of emotional interference that make the experience of happiness, peace, and well-being impossible, or at best, rare. In short, unforgiveness is painful. Break the word *painful* into smaller words, and you get "pay-in-full."

Many are taught from a young age that unforgiveness is sinful and unacceptable. The leverage used to encourage forgiveness has been the fear of retaliation from a judgmental God. As a result, many people claim to have forgiven someone when, in fact, that claim is just empty words, a naïve assertion that forgiveness has happened, or what amounts to lying to one's self.

I'm always amazed at the ever-increasing number of people I encounter in my classes, lectures, or counseling sessions who claim to have forgiven, yet are experiencing an inability to move forward or to feel motivated or enthusiastic about starting a project or pursuing their dreams. They fail to realize or even consider that unforgiveness is the culprit holding them back. They think just telling themselves, "Let it go" or "This isn't important, just ignore it," will do the trick. But when a person is hanging onto deep feelings of anger or self-pity, repeatedly talking about a person in a critical and judgmental way, or deliberately ignoring somebody, they are still plugged into an event from the past that continues to contaminate the present and retard the future. They haven't at all understood what real forgiveness is, how to do it, or how to be sure they have done it.

Many people are up to their necks in unforgiveness, claiming to have nothing to forgive. But if you can recall an incident or a person, or perhaps even something you've regrettably done, and you feel a twinge of anger, hurt, repulsion, or some other negative reaction, there is still forgiving to do.

CHAPTER 2

SO WHAT IS FORGIVENESS ... REALLY?

Your greatest tool for changing your world ...
is your ability to change your mind about the world you behold.
— Phylis Clay Sparks

SIMPLY STATED, TRUE or authentic forgiveness is permanent *emotional detachment.* What is emotional detachment? It's the successful unplugging of what I call an "emotional umbilical cord" attaching us to a person, event, or circumstance that continues to cause emotional distress every time we're reminded of that memory. Being emotionally *attached* or *plugged in* means having a strong "emotional charge" connecting us to what someone did to offend, harm, or otherwise hurt us. These memories sustain their impact by sucking our energy. No wonder so many people feel tired or stressed most of the time!

Now don't misunderstand. I'm not suggesting that it's possible to erase a memory. I'm saying it's entirely possible to emotionally detach *from* that memory and everyone involved, so when that memory is triggered or recalled, it has no power to disturb or interfere with one's happiness and well-being.

Imagine how wonderful it must feel to be free from the emotional reaction to a memory that continually drags you down into anger, resentment, or some other energy-zapping emotion. That memory could be about something that recently happened, or it could be a deeply embedded hurt or regret that happened a long time ago. Think about how it must feel when nothing can disturb your happiness in the present moment, even when reminded of a terrible memory! Consider how incredible it must be to learn *how* to discover and dissolve negative emotional attachments you didn't even realize were lurking in the depths of your subconscious mind!

Still, you may be saying to yourself, "I can't forgive that person! What they did was too terrible. If I forgive, I make what they did okay!" Believe me, that's not the case.

Forgiveness Is Not Condoning

Many people think of forgiveness as condoning someone's unacceptable behavior, letting him or her off the hook. But this perspective keeps one emotionally attached to that person and that memory, which adds up to unforgiveness.

Keep in mind that the value of *true* forgiveness is freeing yourself to fully participate in and enjoy the present moments of life. It's about not being deeply invested in or concerned about someone else getting their just due. Now this doesn't mean backing down when it's appropriate to take a stand, perhaps having to do with your job or some important legal concern. But even that can be done without an "eye for an eye" mentality or desire for retaliation. Trust me when I point out that whomever dishes out ugliness, unkindness, or unfairness will somewhere, somehow get back what they've given out. They will reap what they have sown, and by virtue of Universal Law, which will be explained later in this book, they will draw to them that which is of like kind.

The truth is, we don't need to condone unacceptable behavior, nor do we need to punish ourselves by insisting we have to do something about the situation. What we need to do is unplug mentally and emotionally from that person and their actions. Only by doing this can we ultimately accomplish true forgiveness and the freedom to move on.

Why Is Forgiveness so Important?

I really want you to understand how important true forgiveness is to a happy life. In fact, it's mandatory. But I can hear you saying, "Mandatory!?

That means I *have to* do it! *Why* do I *have to* do it? I don't have to forgive if I don't want to, and *that* person doesn't deserve my forgiveness!" Right on both counts. You don't have to forgive if you don't want to, and the other person might not deserve your forgiveness. But if you really want to *feel good* more of the time and remove the interferences from the flow of good in your life, you must learn about and apply the Forgiveness Process with sincerity and clear intention. You are doing it for you, not them. And as I've already mentioned, you don't have to be concerned about payback. Everyone gets back what they give out according to Universal Law. Keep in mind this includes you, as a result of your own festering and toxic emotional attachments!

Genuine forgiveness is vital because it can free you from unrelenting obstructions to living at higher levels of happiness and well-being. It can free you to enjoy unlimited success and abundance. It can free you from that which might interfere with the health and well-being of your body, mind, and spirit. And last but not least, it can free you to experience the depth and quality of all other relationships in your life.

Remember: emotional attachments suck your vital energy. Think about how many of these emotional umbilical cords you may have attached to people or to negative memories over the course of your lifetime. If you have not emotionally disconnected from them, disempowered them, or dissolved them, they are still sucking your energy, and eventually you will pay with the deterioration of your physical body. This is a big component of aging and disease. By the time most people are fifty years old, many big, fat negative emotional umbilical cords have been sucking their vital energy for so many years that the cells of their bodies have gradually become deficient, deformed, distorted, and dead. That's why people look old, not just because they've reached a certain number of years.

I'd like to emphasize how important your emotional state is in creating your experience of life. Emotions are even more impactful than thoughts, perhaps because they are so involved with ingrained beliefs. Humans come into the world with a built-in *life urge* and a *death urge*, and from that point on, it's a balancing act. When you sink into the denser, thicker emotions, there is less movement of the life force, or energy, and the result is a body and mind that functions with less and less health and vitality.

This means that your entire history of thought, feeling, and belief becomes your consciousness and thereby manifests in your physical form.

There's a terrific book entitled *Molecules of Emotion*, written by Dr. Candice Pert, an internationally recognized pharmacologist. In this book, she explains how the emotions act like drugs in the brain and the body and actually store memories in the cells of the body. She asserts that emotions are chemical ligands, or peptides, that distribute themselves in the body very specifically. This chemical interaction at the cellular level can translate into large changes in behavior, physical activity, and mood, all the result of emotional energy. In Dr. Pert's words, "The body is the unconscious mind!" She goes on to say, "Repressed traumas caused by overwhelming emotion can be stored in a body part, thereafter affecting our ability to feel that part or even move it."

Now rather than try to understand all this, it's enough to say there is scientific evidence behind the fact that emotions are key to the health of our body. Emotions are generated by thoughts, and thoughts are generated by emotions. It seems to be a two-way street. But feelings and emotions carry messages to the individual cells of the body. Because of the time it takes for the negative emotional debris stored in the cells of the body to manifest as illness, deformity, or weakness, must people do not make the connection between past events and present challenges.

For those who think they have nothing to forgive and yet experience health issues, emotions they don't understand, difficulty in pursuing their dreams and goals in life, low self-esteem, and so on, I have included in this book an amazing process called The Soul-Math™ Formula. This unique exercise will help you dig into your history of thoughts, feelings, beliefs, and behavior to reveal and discover old buried "mind viruses." Mind viruses are toxic emotions you may not realize are registered in the cells of your body and are keeping you from moving forward with ease rather than struggle. Although you may not identify with these old buried emotions at this point in your life, they may be playing a very significant role in the choices and decisions you are making or not making. Even unresolved feelings from childhood can still be very active in holding you back, slowly breaking down parts of your body and getting in the way of your ability to clearly connect with that "still small voice within," or your intuitive inner guidance system.

CHAPTER 3

MY PERSONAL STORY

When you forgive, you in no way change the past—
but you sure do change the future.
—Bernard Meltzer

AT THIS POINT, I think it's important to lay the groundwork for launching into the Forgiveness Process about which I'm writing this book by validating it with my own personal story. It's impossible to fully convey the details, or the mental and emotional impact of this experience. Even so, I hope it will help you see that it's possible to detach from and transform even the most devastating or challenging occurrence into a blessing in disguise.

My story goes back many years to a time when a person I respected, trusted, and considered a friend indulged in some shocking behavior about which I will not go into detail. This person exposed a side of themselves that I had not seen before, and needless to say, I was devastated. Suddenly, they began aiming their anger in my direction, literally threatening my life. For weeks I lived in fear about what they might do next.

At some point, I became exhausted from the emotional stress and reached out to a person I considered my spiritual mentor. I spilled my heart out and expressed my need to overcome the terrible haunting fear I was going through. My mentor finally said to me, "Well, how is this person serving you?" What?? How are they serving me? I reacted with surprise and anger instead of seeing his point. I left that session feeling confused and put off, but I kept thinking about that question. I finally sat down with pen and paper and wrote at the top of the page, "How has this person served me?"

It was difficult at first, but slowly my list started to grow and my eyes began to open. It was dawning upon me how depleting and exhausting fear had become to my body, mind, and spirit. I realized that by accepting this person's anger, it now belonged to me. I could see how they were serving me by pushing me to choose strength over weakness and faith over fear. I began to see at a deeper level that things are not always the way they appear on the surface. I realized the importance of stepping back from a challenge and becoming the observer rather than the victim. I was learning how to use my power of imagination to back away and look upon a problem with detached interest, willing to see things from a new and higher perspective. I was cultivating within myself an ability to see beyond appearances.

As my attitude calmed down, I began to understand that everything happens for a reason, that there is good in every person, even those who appear evil. I also began to trust that from that moment on I would be able to see a blessing in every situation, maybe not right away, but eventually I would see it. I also realized that reacting with fear, anger, and resentment do nothing more than pollute one's own body, mind, and spirit.

Finally, my heart began to soften, and I felt ready to transform this person from my adversary to one of my best teachers. What a feeling that was! I could actually see this person from an entirely different perspective! Then it dawned on me. Until this shift happened within me, true forgiveness didn't have a chance.

I still felt shaken and beaten up, but I had to admit that I could see many ways in which I had learned from this experience. I could actually see this person as having served me while still feeling an emotional charge upon what they had done. The beautiful thing was, I felt *willing* and even *ready* to consider totally unplugging from the fear, disappointment, hurt, and shock still attaching me to this person. Perhaps the most important thing I realized is that forgiveness isn't as simple as I had thought.

Having accepted this person as my teacher rather than my adversary, and being willing to continue my journey into forgiveness, I decided to meditate about what to do next. Out of that came a visualization process that enabled me to achieve true forgiveness and freedom. It took me thirty days of repeating this process until I finally unplugged my emotional charge on the memory and achieved a remarkable sense of relief and total freedom from fear. I was able to enjoy that freedom as I went about my daily life without constantly looking over my shoulder. There were no attachments to the memories of what happened other than gratitude for what I had learned.

Things were gliding along at a wonderful pace, but a few months later, the next shoe dropped. My husband suddenly passed away. My "teacher" showed up at the funeral service and presented me with a beautiful handwritten eulogy in honor of my husband, and walked away without saying a word. It was as if everything was brought to final closure. I felt freed at an even deeper level to move on and begin teaching the process I had discovered to others.

CHAPTER 4

GET READY, GET SET ...

*When you hold resentment toward another, you are bound to that
person or condition by an emotional link that is stronger than steel.
Forgiveness is the only way to dissolve that link and get free.*
—Catherine Ponder

NOW THAT I'VE shared with you how the Forgiveness Process
unfolded for me and has since helped numerous others find the
freedom to move on, it's your turn.

Before you start the Process, I have a few suggestions. First of all, have
a journal or pad of paper and pen available. Choose a time when you won't
have to hurry, and find a place where you can sit down, relax, and become
quiet. Next comes the hard part. Turn off your phone! Turn off your
computer and anything else that could disturb, interrupt, or otherwise
distract you.

To help you avoid resistance that can happen as you face the journey
into true forgiveness, take a moment to imagine with me. Take a deep
breath and relax. Now picture yourself standing on a very busy street
corner, wanting to cross to the other side. Looking both ways, you see a
break in the traffic and step off the curb to hurry across. Suddenly, you
hear a voice behind you, yelling, "Don't cross! There's an out-of-control
car coming over the hill!" Quickly, you jump back on the curb, and sure
enough, here comes that car speeding down the street, swerving from

lane to lane. Shaken, you turn to see where that warning voice came from and realize it came from the third-floor window of the building directly behind you.

Obviously, the person in that window had a much broader view of what was happening than you. He saw a much bigger picture. As the one on the street corner, you were only aware of what was happening within your immediate range of vision. Without receiving that warning from the third-story window, you could have made a disastrous choice.

So what's this got to do with forgiveness? Well, before you begin the process, it helps to get a broader perspective of the situation. Go to your own third-story window. Do this by using your power of thought to step into that part of you I call the *Observer*. This is simply a mental and emotional shift to a viewing point of detached interest, where you feel more willing to start unplugging the emotional umbilical cords that have been anchoring you in fear, anger, and unhappiness. It's not an attitude of coolness, indifference, or emotional isolation. It's simply the art of watching the drama of life from a neutral, higher perspective. Almost like watching a movie. It's the perfect place from which to make wise choices while at the same time being involved with life in the midst of whatever current situation is happening.

Okay. Now you've stepped up to the starting line. Get ready, get set ... GO!

CHAPTER 5

THE FORGIVENESS PROCESS: FORGIVING OTHERS

Forgive, not because they deserve forgiveness, but because you deserve peace.
—Author Unknown

Step One: Take Time to Consider Who You Need to Forgive.

In all likelihood you already have someone in mind. You may have a number of people in mind. That's okay. Just pick one, maybe the one who really gets to you. The rest can wait. Once you've moved through the Process and feel the freedom of having successfully forgiven that one person, you can move on to the others. And you know what? The Process will become easier each time you do it! How great is that? In fact, after you have worked through the Forgiveness Process a few times, you may find true forgiveness as easy as "letting it roll off your back" with respect to some people.

One other thing. The person you forgive may currently be in your life, or it may be someone out of your past, even from your childhood. It could be someone who is deceased. None of these things matter. What matters is the emotional charge you feel attaching you to them. It is still very much alive and present in your body, mind, and spirit. So don't think that because they're no longer around, or you never see them, you don't need to unplug from them.

Step Two: Ask Yourself: "Am I truly *ready* and *willing* to detach, unplug, and move on?"

The answer to this question may not be all that simple. So before you check this step off your list and move on to the next one, do some deep soul-searching. I suggest using a journal for this step. Writing out your thoughts can really help you get to the truth of the matter. And that's important.

I have counseled with many people who say they are ready to forgive and maybe think they have already forgiven someone. Yet they still feel hurt or angry every time the memory of that person is triggered. The thing is, they don't realize how addicted they've become to these hurt and angry feelings, or to feelings of resentment, victimhood, or other toxic emotions that keep them plugged into that memory and that person. Much like an addiction to alcohol or drugs, these deeply embedded feelings can be very hard to break. Many people don't realize their demand for justice and restitution keeps them stuck in an emotional fog that's become their distorted version of *normal*, or even *comfortable*. You read that right! Many people become amazingly comfortable in their misery.

So how do you know if this is true for you? Take note of how you feel and react when you recall a particular memory about someone. Do you feel anger or self-pity? Do you talk about that person behind their back? Does being with that person upset you? Do you retell the dramatic story about how they wronged you over and over again? Guess what? You may not be ready or willing to set yourself free. The problem is, for every moment you spend replaying some hurtful event, whether verbally or mentally, you are digging an even deeper hole of distress and frustration for yourself! You may even feel as though you're wearing lead boots, stepping from one puddle of sticky tar into the next, while your zest for life and happiness declines.

As you can see, it is *vitally* important to be in a state of *readiness* and *willingness* in order to even begin to truly forgive. Otherwise, you are deceiving yourself and real forgiveness will not be possible. Readiness and willingness represent your conscious choice to be free and to devote your present moments to choosing constructive, happy thoughts and feelings. So are you *really* ready and willing to forgive? If so, let's move on. But in the event just the thought of unplugging your anger from this person makes you even angrier, you might want to start with someone to whom you have an emotional umbilical cord attached that's smaller in diameter. Remember: you must be *ready* to detach and move on. Believe me, Universal Law will settle the score. You don't have to.

Step Three: Describe Your Grievance.

Okay, you know who you need to forgive and are truly ready to let go of any emotional attachment to them and the memory of what they did. Now, write their name at the top of a journal page. Remember, this is *your* journal. No one needs to see this but you. Now under that name describe in detail what happened, how you felt as it happened, how you felt after it happened, and where it stands now. Spend some time with this. You could even take a few days to be sure you have spilled it all out on paper. And believe me, sometimes it takes a lot of time and paper, but it's worth it!

Step Four: List the Ways This Person Has Served You.

This may seem impossible, considering what this person did to you or to someone you love. But trust me, they *did* actually serve you in some way. However, if you're having a problem with this, here are some ideas that might help you get started.

This person
- gave me an opportunity to learn true forgiveness.
- helped me see how opinionated I can be.
- showed me how devastating such actions can be to another person.
- helped me bring old hurts to a conscious level to be healed and released.
- reflected back to me the same thing I did to someone else. (Wow, that's a big one!)
- helped me learn to deflect negativity aimed at me.
- taught me that I don't have to accept what someone tries to give me.
- taught me how energy-zapping and distracting a grudge can be.
- helped me see that it isn't my job to punish someone. They will take care of that themselves.

Now keep going! As with all of the steps in the Forgiveness Process, don't rush it. Take several days if necessary. It's important to be thorough at this stage. If you take your time, you could be quite surprised at what occurs to you. This is especially true if it happened a long time ago. Time may allow you to more clearly see some of the lessons you've learned as a result of this person's actions. And don't be concerned that by doing this you're making what that person did okay. You're not. Just remember, in time it will become evident that everyone eventually reaps what they've sown.

Step Five: When You Feel Complete with Your List, Notice What's Happening.

You will know when your list is complete. How will you know? Because you'll notice that your heart is softening toward the other person. In fact, you may be surprised that you have started to see them through new eyes and from a different perspective. This person is looking more and more like your teacher rather than your adversary. This doesn't mean you have to *like* your teacher, but at the very least, you will begin to acknowledge the value of what he or she taught you or pointed out to you. The lessons you have learned are outweighing the grievances. What a wonderful thing to feel as this transformation takes place.

Now you are ready to *unplug* the emotional umbilical cord for good! Now you are ready to free yourself to move on and to free the other person to face a judge and jury that does not include you!

Step Six: Completing the Process.

It's time to unplug that cord for good and dismiss your teacher! We're going to do this using a simple meditation technique to calm the body and focus the mind, along with visualization to guide you into the healing freedom of true forgiveness. Why visualization? Because mental imagery is a powerful use of the mind to create intentional desires or goals in your world of experience. Not only that, it feels great!

Ready? Here we go.

Find a quiet place where you won't be disturbed. Sit in a comfortable position, close your eyes, and start with slow, deep breaths and calming thoughts as you progressively relax your body. Begin with your face and head and then move all the way down to your feet. If you are a meditator, you may already have a technique that works for you. If you are not a meditator, once your body is relaxed, continue to quiet your mind by using a word like *peace* over and over, slower and slower, as you breathe deeply and relax more and more.

Now use your power of imagination to visualize yourself standing in a beautiful place in nature, perhaps a quiet beach, a secluded forest, or a mountaintop; anywhere you'd enjoy spending time. Give it color and detail, making it as real as you can. Notice the beauty all around you.

When you're ready, imagine the person you've been journaling about appearing in the distance. See them walking toward you until the two of you are standing face-to-face. Reach out and take their hands in yours. Look into their eyes. Say to him or her, "Thank you for teaching me (guiding me, showing me). You can stop now, because I have learned the lesson(s). I now release you. You are free to leave."

Imagine letting go of their hands and gently turning them around. Now watch them walk away. The goal in this part of the visualization is for them to continue walking away from you until they disappear in the distance. Releasing this person in your mind's eye is like releasing them from a contract, a contract to serve you. Once you have learned the lesson, the contract has been fulfilled. It's over. When they have disappeared in the distance, it's as if the contract has been officially torn up. But please note; depending on how large and strong the emotional umbilical cord is that has attached the two of you, this visualization may need to be repeated several times before this person disappears from sight, indicating that the cord is finally unplugged.

When I developed this process in the midst of my own traumatic situation, it took thirty days before my teacher vanished out of sight. I went back to that place in my mind every day, picking up where I left off the day before, and continuing to watch this person walk farther and farther away from me. Sometimes he'd look back, and sometimes he'd stop. Sometimes my mind would start wandering off, thinking about what I might have for lunch or dinner. That's when I'd go back to my daily routine and just repeat the process the next day. So when you notice your logical mind beginning to think about other things, stop and go about your daily business. Then go back the next day and repeat the process. Eventually, you will see that person walk off and completely disappear. That's when you'll know you've truly unplugged the emotional umbilical cord, and you'll feel the joy and freedom of true forgiveness. Then go ahead and laugh, sing, and jump up and down! Express yourself in whatever joyful manner you choose. You've just accomplished something great! And from now on, whenever that person or the memory of what happened comes to mind, it will be just that—a memory and nothing else.

Keep in mind, though, that even when authentic forgiveness has happened, nothing will necessarily have changed in the physical dimension. Your boss will still be your boss, your mate will still be your mate, a person who betrayed or abandoned you will still be gone, and so on. But you will feel unbelievable freedom. And if this person is still a part of your life, don't be surprised if how they treat you changes for the better, or that one day they magically slide out your life. This is a world of cause and effect, and what you have done by applying the Forgiveness Process is set new cause into motion. That means there will be some effect in your human experience in response to that cause.

The beautiful thing is, the memory of what happened will no longer haunt you. That means you'll never be triggered to relive it again as if it were happening right now. And you'll never recreate that same lesson delivered by somebody else because the lesson is already learned.

Okay, so you've taken the necessary time to go through the journaling process and have repeated the visualization until the person you've been mentally and emotionally attached to has walked away in your mind's eye and has disappeared in the distance. You have unplugged and honestly feel they can no longer have any negative effect on you. But what if you feel somewhat confused because you still don't feel quite right about the situation? What if you don't feel the peace that should come with true, authentic forgiveness? In that case, you need to rethink who else you need to forgive. Journaling will help with this. And by the way, that person may just be yourself! That's right. You may need forgiving too! We'll discuss that in the next chapter.

CHAPTER 6

THE FORGIVENESS PROCESS: FORGIVING YOURSELF

It's toughest to forgive ourselves. So it's probably best to start with other people. It's almost like peeling an onion. Layer by layer, forgiving others, you really do get to the point where you can forgive yourself.
—Patty Duke

SO HOW DO you know you need to forgive yourself? The same way you know you need to forgive someone else. You notice an emotional charge whenever you recall an incident where you might have hurt someone, made a regretful decision, or failed to do something you promised to do. But self-forgiveness can be a bit tricky. In fact, you may not even realize you've done anything that needs forgiving.

So how is this even possible? Well, you might have done something so long ago that you no longer remember it. But your subconscious mind never forgets. It stores that memory, and you carry the self-blame, shame, or guilt with you until it's discovered and forgiven. If you carry with you a lot of regret about things you did in the past that haven't been corrected, healed, or forgiven, you will sink deeper and deeper into low self-worth and self-denial, pushing away or ignoring many of the good things in life.

Forgiving yourself requires a much different perspective than forgiving someone else. That's because you have to ask the question "How did I serve myself?" It's a tough question to answer. But it really needs to be addressed if you want to stop beating yourself up over something you said or did and move forward in your life. So if you're ready, let's get started.

Step One: Take Time to Consider Why You May Need to Forgive Yourself.

The journey toward self-forgiveness begins by realizing the part you played in a past event, even though you may have already forgiven everyone else concerned. Emotionally unplugging from the memory and from the self that you were at the time you participated in such an event is vitally important to your health, happiness, and future success.

Self-remorse, self-condemnation, regret, shame, or blame could be lurking in the back of your mind, keeping you stuck in low self-worth and holding you back from pursuing your dreams. Just facing this fact is enough reason why you must apply the Forgiveness Process to yourself.

Step Two: Ask Yourself: "Am I truly *ready* and *willing* to detach, unplug, and move on?"

Self-forgiveness can't happen until you're ready to take personal responsibility. Being *ready* to do this starts with laying aside self-pity or the stubborn need to be right, and realizing how damaging self-judgment has been to your happiness and well-being.

You may be stunned at how much personal courage, creativity, strength, and clarity about your own goals and objectives begins to stir within you by admitting that self-forgiveness must happen. Just declaring yourself *ready* to do the work it takes to reclaim your right to a happy life will begin to lift your self-acceptance to higher and higher levels.

Are you *ready* and willing to truly forgive yourself and become the self-confident, positive, and happy person you were meant to be? Then move on to Step Three!

Step Three: Describe Your Grievance.

In order to make self-forgiveness as clear as possible, let's use a specific example. Since many of us have felt the sting of abandonment as someone left our life, let's use abandonment as an example. Let's say *you* abandoned someone and have some blame, shame, or guilt lingering in the background of your consciousness about what you did. If this example doesn't apply to you, play along with me and pretend so you see how to clear emotional debris about yourself having to do with any situation.

Now, just as in the Forgiveness Process about someone else, turn your attention toward your own thoughts and feelings. Think about a time when you walked out of someone's life without caring how they felt or because you simply couldn't stay any longer. Write down in detail what happened, how you felt as it happened, and where it stands now. Take your time doing this because sometimes it's deeply painful to relive a memory for which you have subconsciously blamed yourself. Take a few days to be sure you have poured it all out on paper. Don't hold back! Believe me, down the road you'll be glad you shook those emotional umbilical cords and unplugged them from your former self!

Step Four: List the Ways You Have Served Yourself by Doing What You Did.

This is not easy to do. In fact, you might find yourself with pen in hand just staring at a blank sheet of paper for a long time. "How did I serve myself? Wow. What a silly question. I hurt this person by leaving them behind, and I'm supposed to see how I served myself by doing what I did?"

It's okay! Your reaction is normal. The first answer that often comes to someone's mind is "I didn't serve myself! I damaged myself! I hate myself for doing what I did the way I did it!" Or "I'm the one who was hurt and unhappy. How could leaving that situation possibly be my fault?"

Okay, let's move on. Stop staring at the paper and start writing. Just pretend that sometime in the past you thoughtlessly abandoned someone. Here are some ideas to help you get started with thinking about the possibilities.

I served myself by
- forcing myself to see that I must always move out of relationships with compassion.

- learning I must treat myself and others with kindness as I stand strong in the truth of my decisions and actions.
- realizing how I carelessly treated someone else is helping me forgive those who abandoned me.
- being willing to see the lesson I was unconsciously teaching myself by demonstrating my own immaturity and selfishness.
- seeing I was acting out my own flaws, revealing my own level of self-worth at the time.
- realizing it's okay to be compassionate with myself and accept what happened as a steppingstone to a higher sense of compassion and moral character.

Keep going and don't rush it. Take your time with this. You may even realize how easy it is to forgive yourself for feelings you had just by realizing you felt them! They may simply have been immature reactions in situations you didn't know how to handle at that time in your life. Just by realizing they have nothing to do with the person you are today may be enough to easily let them go and free you from their lingering effects. Don't you wish all forgiveness was that simple?

Step Five: When You Feel Complete with Your List, Notice What's Happening.

It will become obvious to you when your list is complete because you will start recognizing the teacher in you rather than the self-saboteur. Be willing to honor yourself in that way! Honor the lessons you have learned that are making you a better person now. And, as in the process for forgiving others, you are now ready to actually unplug the emotional umbilical cord from those memories for good! It's time to free yourself in gratitude for the self-instruction.

Step Six: Completing the Process.

Now it's time to unplug for good and go forward, being the best you that you can be! Just as in the process for forgiving others, we're going to do a simple meditation technique to calm your body and focus your mind, along with a visualization to move you into the freedom of authentic self-forgiveness. Visualization is a powerful way to unplug from negative and harmful emotional attachments to the past.

Ready? Here we go.

Find a quiet place where you won't be disturbed. Sit comfortably as you close your eyes and start taking slow, deep breaths. Focus your mind on calming thoughts as you progressively relax your entire body from head to toe. If you are used to meditating, you may have a technique that works for you. If not, once your body is relaxed, continue to calm your mind and body by using a word like *peace* over and over as you breathe deeply and continue to relax.

Now visualize yourself standing in a beautiful place, perhaps a cliff overlooking the ocean, a lovely garden, or in your own backyard; anywhere you'd enjoy spending time. Notice all the color and natural beauty around you.

Now imagine your former self walking toward you until the two of you stand face-to-face. (If it was in the distant past, imagine seeing yourself at that age.) Reach out and take your own hands, like reaching into a mirror, and look into your own eyes. Say to yourself, "Thank you for teaching me (guiding me, showing me). You can stop now. I've learned the lesson. I now free you to leave."

Then imagine gently turning your former self around and watching the other you walk away. The goal in this part of the visualization is to see your former self continue walking away from you, eventually disappearing in the distance. This is like releasing your former self from a contract, a contract to make you a stronger, happier, wiser, and more compassionate person. Once you've learned the lesson, the contract has successfully been completed. When your former self has disappeared in the distance, the emotional umbilical cord has been unplugged. It may require doing this several times before the other you disappears from sight, depending on how large and strong the emotional umbilical cord is attaching the two of you.

Once you free yourself from the emotional charge of your own actions, you will automatically begin to focus upon the good in your life, the people who care about you, and the new friends you have made and are attracting into your life, rather than noticing only those who are no longer there.

Also, realize that people are always changing, so when someone leaves you in the future, don't take it personally. Likewise, you are always changing. So when you find yourself having outgrown a relationship, or for some unselfish reason know it's time to move out of someone's life, take that action with compassion, courage, and a willingness to say good-bye while wanting the highest and best for the other person and everyone involved. Then walk away into the freedom by accepting change, evolution, and the next experience of life with a sense of peace and well-being.

Remember, this example had to do with abandonment issues. Keep in mind that it will work with any negative feelings you have held onto about yourself and something you might have done that you perceive as cruel or wrong. Notice as you look back that you were just being yourself and doing the best you knew how to do at the time.

CHAPTER 7

SUSTAINING TRUE FORGIVENESS

Forgiveness does not change the past, but it does enlarge the future.
—Paul Boese

SUSTAINING TRUE FORGIVENESS can be tricky and difficult if the person who caused you distress is still in your life, for instance a spouse, relative, coworker, boss, or even a close friend you really don't want to lose. If they continually hurl insults or critical judgments at you, and you have truly unplugged from what they have done in the past, you need to make sure you have forgiven yourself for your past reactions. Don't fall into the trap of repeating those hurtful reactions. All this does is create another emotional umbilical cord, and you really don't want to go through that again, do you? My suggestion is to have a positive affirmation ready to help block any negativity they may send your way. This will help keep it from gaining a foothold in your thoughts and feelings. I'll show you how to construct effective affirmations later. Right now, just know that if you have sincerely and genuinely severed the emotional umbilical cord attaching you to that person, one of the three following things may happen:

1. Your love or respect for that person may overshadow any temptation to react in a negative way to what they're saying or doing. You'll maintain a detached understanding that the other person is simply venting something lurking deep inside and it needs an outlet.

You're just a convenient target because they know you won't go away. If necessary, imagine a shield of light around you deflecting the negative words and attitude aimed in your direction. (This really helps!)

2. You may have the courage to take a stand and, with compassionate intention, tell that person their words and actions toward you are unacceptable. You may even suggest calmly discussing your line of acceptability and where it might lead that relationship. Let the freedom of true forgiveness build your self-esteem and give you the courage to stand up for yourself in a non-vindictive and open-minded way, and be ready and willing to leave that situation if necessary. Forgiveness does not mean becoming another person's whipping post.

3. When tempted to react to another person's words or actions, you will stop yourself from giving up by remembering that you have set a new cause into motion with authentic forgiveness. You will find yourself more patient, allowing the time necessary for a solution you may not have expected to unfold. This solution may be a change in the other person's attitude and behavior, a new job in a new place, or an easy and peaceful departure by the other person from your life.

What about the Act of Betrayal?

Forgiving is rediscovering the shining path of peace
that at first you thought others took away when they betrayed you.
—Dodinsky

One of the most difficult experiences anyone can live through is an act of betrayal. Betrayal is the violation of trust within a relationship, group, or organization. It has many degrees of severity, often described as dishonesty, backstabbing, deception, infidelity, and even treachery, to name a few. But whatever descriptive you use, the results are the same:

painful psychological and emotional reactions, leading you directly into the land of unforgiveness.

When you feel betrayed, you may go through many of the same emotions associated with grief. That's because an act of betrayal causes something to die, break apart, or fall into pieces. It could be your self-worth, comfort zone, plans for the future, relationship, or sense of security. This sudden change can plunge you into the bottomless pit of devastation, denial, isolation, and even depression, all of which can lead to prolonged anger, blame, resentment, and unforgiveness.

But here's something to consider. What if the experience of betrayal turns out to be a catalyst for positive change? What if it serves to shake us loose from old, worn-out ways of thinking and being and forces us to move beyond people and situations that no longer serve our highest good? Perhaps we have worked for the same company for many years, depending upon that job to take us into retirement, only to become the victim of corporate downsizing. Or maybe we married someone we planned to be partnered with for life, but several years into the marriage, he or she announces that he or she is leaving. Maybe a person we thought of as a close friend betrays us by putting a picture of something very private to us on social media.

Yes, these are acts of betrayal in the ordinary sense of the word. But as long as we continue to think of them as betrayals, we will suffer through years of pain and loss of energy, not to mention a very dark form of unforgiveness. As difficult as it may be, if we can open ourselves to see these experiences as change agents for good, we can stop grieving over that which has broken apart and instead build something brand-new!

There comes a point in our own consciousness evolution when it's time to think for ourselves, to become self-conscious instead of group conscious, to move beyond fear into trust. But because many of us dread change, we don't pay attention to the signals and inner urges to make a change. We then stay stuck in old, familiar patterns of belief, clinging to people and situations that have essentially ended.

Here's an example. Let's say you feel a growing desire to leave your job. The desire intensifies, but you ignore it because you are unsure about what to do next. Anxiety and tension mount as you battle with your desire to leave by saying things like "What would my family think of me if I gave up this job?" Or "It's not the right time. I'll just make the best of it." Or "Things are bound to improve if I just hang in there." But months go by and nothing changes except your accelerating anger and resentment, not only about being in a job you don't want to be in but also toward those you work with and toward yourself for not having the courage to do something about it.

Eventually, because of your unhappiness, you begin to manifest illness in your body, perhaps ulcers or headaches. You become less productive, less creative, less cooperative, less interested. Then when you finally get laid off or fired, you perceive it as betrayal.

But what if you learned to *reframe* the experience of betrayal into a symbolic event in your life, forcing you to face, forgive, and move through the ending, separation, symbolic death and into emotional release, new awareness, and rebirth? What if you trusted your inner guidance and could see the experience as fertile ground for personal growth and evolution?

Betrayal is always a shock from the human perspective, and the grief and pain associated with it can amplify a sense of emptiness, loneliness, meaninglessness, and futility. But if we learn to look beyond the appearance, we can see the betrayer as the initiator of our own evolution of something new, something better. To free ourselves from feelings brought on by an act of betrayal, we must learn to see the betrayer as our teacher, our nudger, a blessing in disguise, and allow the experience to stir a willingness to begin the Forgiveness Process. And forgive we must. Unforgiveness will keep us stuck in the grieving process—a very dark place to spend time.

I'm suggesting that you do your best to see all your betrayal experiences through the lens of higher awareness and view them as powerful turning points that can lead you into greater fulfillment and happiness. I'm suggesting you see your betrayer as someone wearing his or her angel wings to force you back on purpose, move you out of something that doesn't serve your highest good, bolster your strength and faith, or help you teach someone else about the power of true forgiveness.

Let Universal Laws Take Over!

One of the biggest blocks to forgiveness for many people is the demand that justice be served. They can't get beyond the idea that forgiveness is letting a person off the hook for some terrible thing they did. And when that terrible thing involves a criminal act, such as child abuse, murder, stealing, or some other unacceptable act of violence, there's no question that true forgiveness can seem impossible.

But keep in mind that human laws involving the judicial process, courtrooms, punishment, perhaps jail, and even the death penalty are *not* the only set of rules active in this world. There are Universal Laws that are in constant operation for everyone at all times. These laws operate in response to our use of emotional, mental, and physical energy. When our thoughts, feelings, beliefs, and behavior violate or fall out of alignment with noble motives and intention, Universal Law will see to it that we pay the piper. Likewise, when we behave with kindness, compassion, and so on, these laws support us with the rewards of peace, abundance, internal guidance, strength, and all good things.

I'm sure you've heard the phrase, "You reap what you sow." This is the *Law of Cause and Effect.* In other words, you tend to get back what you give out. This reciprocal law is obvious when someone treats you the same way you treated him or her. But that behavior can also come from someone else. In other words, if you throw a boomerang at someone, it may come back to you from a completely different direction.

Another Universal Law to be mindful about is the *Law of Attraction.* This energy-driven law is similar to the Law of Cause and Effect but acts more like magnetic energy. Your thought-and-feeling atmosphere that motivates behavior will tend to magnetize and draw to you that which matches your consciousness. So if you desire peace, you must "be" peace. If you desire prosperity, you must cultivate a consciousness of prosperity. It is also true, based on this law, that you are always exactly where your consciousness places you.

As a teenager in high school, I learned a good lesson about how the Law of Attraction works. There was this girl who just bothered me. I reacted to her rumpled appearance, the way she ate with her mouth open, what I saw as her obnoxious personality, and the fact that she liked me! As a result, every time I turned around, guess who was there? It was the Law of Attraction in action!

One day I was in the girls' bathroom at school, and she walked in right behind me. As we both stood in front of the sinks, I looked at her reflection in the mirror and suddenly realized something had to change. It became clear to me that what had to change was my attitude. My attitude was gluing her to me. I knew that changing my feelings about her wouldn't be easy, so I decided to change my thoughts first.

I remembered a profound statement made to me by my Sunday school teacher, which I have never forgotten. When I told her about a difficult situation in my life, her response was "Phylis, just love your way out of it!" So I started allowing love to take place in my thoughts and as best I could in my feelings. I tried looking at this girl in the mirror through the eyes of love instead of loathing, and I began to see someone different.

The next thing I knew, I was smiling at her. Then I asked how she was doing and actually started a conversation. The interesting thing was, as I allowed kind thoughts and feelings of acceptance to move out of me instead of judgment and repulsion, the conversation became easier. But the *really* interesting thing was, after I changed my attitude, I rarely saw this girl anymore. I had unglued myself by changing my thoughts and feelings to something positive. By doing so, I loved my way out of that unforgiving pit of judgment and superiority and found myself feeling something different for this girl.

Years later, as I reflected back on this incident, I realized this girl was wearing her angel wings, showing up to teach me about love and compassion. As a result of my taking responsibility to love in that one incident, I have avoided many opportunities to fall into holes of critical judgment and arrogance over the years. And because of what I call an "angel encounter," I believe I have had a much happier and joy-filled experience on my journey of life.

The truth is, we are each responsible for all of our experiences of life. Did you get that? It's really important that you do. We are responsible for all of our experiences *of* life, not our experiences *in* life. In other words, we aren't responsible for everything that happens to us, but we are responsible for how we react to what happens. So you see, it's totally under our control. Life just happens. How we react to it is up to us.

Yet another Universal Law is the *Law of Circulation*, sometimes called the *Law of Giving and Receiving*. This is a real butt-kicker because it calls attention to the fact that when you forget or refuse to give, you get shortchanged on the receiving end. Likewise, if you over-give, perhaps out of a need for attention, or you think you don't deserve to receive, you also get shortchanged on the receiving end. The trick to being in compliance with this law is to balance your giving and receiving. Be open and willing to receive so that you replenish and have plenty to share. Then give of what you have with no conditions attached.

It's amazing to me how many people have shut down on the receiving half of the giving-receiving cycle. Because of their low self-worth or desire for attention, some people over-give and refuse to accept acts of kindness from other people. Their over-giving might involve caretaking, money, possessions, time, or energy. If not replenished by being open to receive, they will deplete their resources as well as their physical and mental energy, and this often results in feelings of victimhood and self-pity, or even physical illness. Learning to achieve a balance between giving and receiving is mandatory to a balanced expression of life. Now this doesn't mean holding back with respect to giving; it simply means lifting one's self-worth to a place of simply saying thank you when someone sends good your way.

The last law I will mention is the *Law of Reflection*. This is often referred to as mirroring. It's not much different from the other laws, but it can give you a very clear idea about how people, situations, and circumstances are always acting like a mirror, reflecting back to you something about yourself, your beliefs, and your behavior.

Now here's a point I want to drive home with respect to forgiveness as it relates to the laws of the Universe. Most of the time, people get stuck on what someone else did to them that was unkind, hurtful, or worse. But just as often, people are stuck in self-blame and guilt about something they did to someone else that is making their lives miserable as they relive the regretful memory over and over. Just keep in mind that when you think you need to forgive yourself, you just might have been unconsciously holding a mirror up for someone else! This means that whatever dastardly thing you did could be reflecting back to someone else his or her own awful actions. So you might have been showing up as a teacher for that person. Does that excuse your bad behavior? No. But it makes it easier for you to understand why you might have done what you did and thereby makes self-forgiveness a lot simpler.

Don't ever forget that the laws of the Universe operate both ways. Sometimes you're the student, and sometimes you play the role of teacher. So if someone treats you badly, remember, they could be holding the mirror up for you and offering you an opportunity to practice the art of true forgiveness.

The Mind/Body Connection ... and What It Has to Do with Forgiveness

It's now commonly accepted in the medical profession that mental and emotional stress can affect our health on many levels. This is referred to as the mind/body connection and might show up as changes in blood pressure, stomach ulcers, or as some other physical indicator that something may be emotionally out of balance.

Don't ever forget that prolonged feelings of hurt, self-pity, anger, resentment, desire for revenge, blame, shame, or guilt can become toxic in the body, mind, and spirit. This is true whether you're conscious of these feelings or they lay buried in your subconscious mind from long ago. Repetitive negative thoughts and emotional reactions will eventually scream warnings from the body and simply add to your misery.

A good clue as to whether or not you have achieved genuine forgiveness might be in noticing how often you tell your story about a person who has wronged you or how often you find yourself thinking about it and reliving it over and over in your mind. If you have achieved credible forgiveness, you will find yourself focused in the present moment rather than the past. You will have learned to choose peace instead of being drawn into threatening thoughts or emotions that disturb that peace.

Previously, I referred to the work of Dr. Candace Pert who presented her research in *Molecules of Emotion*. Dr. Pert describes how our emotions can register in very specific areas of the body, affecting one's general level of mental and physical health and well-being.

This concept has been taken to very specific levels by an increasing numbers of authors, including Louise Hay. In her book *Heal Your Body*, which is based upon her personal experience and many other similar cases, she links unresolved emotions to specific conditions of the body and suggests what must change in a person's thoughts and feelings in order to improve their physical health.

In a wonderful book entitled *Accidental Cure*, Dr. Simon Yu discusses his personal journey from practicing medicine in a traditional fashion, focusing upon treating symptoms of disease with medications to finally realizing that "the medications never correct the underlying problems and each medication creates its own side effects that require other medications." Such underlying problems, according to Dr. Yu, could be parasite infections, heavy metal toxicity, food allergies, dental problems, or even unresolved emotional states. He makes the following statement:

> Many "incurable patients" need an honest self-evaluation, as well as counseling, to assess their inner conflict with their body, mind, and spirit. Their incurable medical conditions may have originated as unresolved emotional states from childhood, or possibly dead-end marriages or careers. This does not mean "it is all in their heads." However, patients' emotional states affect their health, and unresolved conflicts are embedded in every cell of their bodies (100 trillion cells), resonating and manifesting in their organs.

I have personally demonstrated the mind/body connection in my own life a number of times. As a child and on into adulthood, I suffered with severe asthma and allergies. Since discovering the Forgiveness Process and The Soul-Math Formula (which we'll talk about in-depth in later chapters), I was able to reveal deeply buried emotional imprints, bring them to a conscious level, and take the appropriate steps to forgive and free myself from the burdens I'd been carrying for so many years. I was then led to exactly the right actions to take, which have healed the asthma and greatly reduced the allergic reactions.

The interesting thing to me is how unaware I was of the negative emotional imprints I carried in the cells of my body. I happen to be a patient at Prevention and Healing, the alternative medical practice of Dr. Simon Yu. After conducting an acupuncture meridian assessment for me during one of my office visits, he reported to me that my gallbladder meridian was weak. He then handed me a paper entitled "Unresolved Feelings and Their Target Organs." Listed under the word *gallbladder* were four emotions: resentment, victimhood, bitterness, and blaming. I was stunned. In no way could I identify with these terrible emotions. I put that paper aside and forgot about it. Then about two years later, I experienced severe abdominal pain that resulted in surgical removal of my gallbladder. A week or so after surgery, I was sitting in my office and glanced over at a stack of papers on a bookshelf. One paper was sticking out about two inches from the rest. I pulled on it, and there was the paper Dr. Yu had given me two years earlier. That's when I realized I had to get serious about exploring these subconscious emotions. I worked The Soul-Math Formula, an amazing process to help uncover buried feelings and beliefs, and realized these emotions had nothing to do with who I am now but everything to do with my childhood.

I was a very shy child. When I tell people that, they're reluctant to believe me. In fact, I was quite shy into early adulthood, and even today I feel my shyness on occasion. I was an only child, and my mother was very caring and protective of her fragile little girl. My mom was an undeniable extrovert, quite the opposite of her extremely shy child. During this exploration, I realized as that shy little girl I felt like a victim of my mother's control. I resented having to manipulate her to get what I wanted by dropping hints and waiting until she thought it was her idea. I'm sure I felt bitterness and must have blamed her for all the "smother love" she doled out. Now don't get the wrong idea. My mother was wonderful. She devoted her life to loving me, caring for me, and supporting me. But as a painfully shy child, I didn't understand that. So here I was, many years later, experiencing the outcome of emotions I didn't realize had become "mind viruses" in the cells of my body. I still had a lot of forgiving to do: of myself and of the child who no longer existed except as the unforgiven emotional residue registered in specific parts of my adult body.

This experience awakened me more than ever as to how easy it is to think we have nothing more to forgive and how common it is to stay in denial about unconscious, unresolved feelings and beliefs causing our bodies to scream for freedom.

So You Think You Have Nothing to Forgive??

I have talked with many people who think they have nothing or no one to forgive, and yet they are weighed down by feelings they don't understand; feelings holding them back from moving forward with ease rather than struggle. Some have sworn up and down that they have already forgiven everyone and everything that called for forgiveness. Even those who have recognized an obvious forgiveness challenge and have applied the Forgiveness Process as outlined in this book can still feel an emotional drag that they don't understand. Oh, they might feel mentally and emotionally free with respect to a person or situation to which they applied the Process, and yet they complain about being frozen and unable to move on with definite intention and self-confidence.

If you have experienced feelings causing you to remain stuck in hesitation or doubt, unable to find the courage to make new choices, or take a risk in order to move on with your life, you may be anchored down in low levels of self-worth. Unworthiness will cause you to deny or push away the flow of good in your life. If you are afraid to move forward with your dreams and desires and repeatedly deny your own happiness, you are more than likely dealing with self-blame, shame, guilt, regret, or some belief about yourself that might have been taught to you by someone else. If you can dig back in time and recall an incident, a person, or something that you yourself did and feel a twinge of guilt, hurt, self-pity, or avoidance about thinking of it at all, there may be toxic emotions buried in the deepest corners of your subconscious mind and in the cells of your body crying out to be recognized and forgiven.

One of the biggest clues pointing to suppressed negative feelings about yourself or something you did in the past is the condition of your body. Your physical body is a powerful feedback system. Have you had illness, pain, or some unwanted condition manifest in your body? If so, investigate the possible mental/emotional cause behind that condition. Like me, you may be experiencing the physical results of unconscious childhood emotional reactions.

Let's say your body is generally healthy, perhaps because you are young enough that toxic, unresolved emotions haven't yet caused a physical problem. There will still be plenty of clues available letting you know that something is amiss. This is where The Soul-Math Formula enters the picture. This is an amazing process to help you dig out feelings that you have pushed down, denied, and forgotten about. The thing is, these feelings are still alive and lurking in the back of your mind and in the cells of your body. The Soul-Math Formula will help you reveal that which you had no idea has been controlling your life.

PART 2

DIAGNOSING AND CORRECTING PROBLEMS WITH THE SOUL-MATH™ FORMULA

The final mystery is oneself.
When one has weighed the sun in the balance,
and measured the steps of the moon
and mapped out the seven heavens star by star,
there still remains oneself.
—Oscar Wilde

CHAPTER 8

GET READY TO FACE THE FACTS!

You never find yourself until you face the truth.
—Pearl Bailey

I**F YOU ARE** ready to experience more of life and to be happier, more prosperous, healthier, loving, and lovable, a new game plan may be required. I'm sure you've heard the saying, "If you keep doing what you've been doing, you'll keep getting what you've been getting!" If you find yourself desiring to improve, expand, and more fully enjoy life, something has to change. The Soul-Math Formula can help you discover what those changes must be and how to make them.

This formula is both a diagnostic and corrective tool that can help you systematically uncover and understand the mental and emotional habit patterns motivating your choices and decisions, most of the time unconsciously. You may think you have nothing to forgive, but The Soul-Math Formula will assist you in exploring and bringing to the surface those unforgiven and unexplained feelings, fears, phobias, and childhood traumas that still influence your choices, power of will, and general behavior in everyday life.

Work the formula as if you were on an archeological dig into the deepest, darkest corners of your psyche. If you are honest with yourself, you will unearth those buried beliefs that have caused you to make your life decisions up until now. Once that happens, you will know exactly what needs forgiving and can then apply the Forgiveness Process to free yourself at last!

As you make the changes revealed to you, you will be amazed at the courage you bring forth to let go of old addictive behaviors to explore new ideas and pursue your dreams without hesitation. You will honor yourself more and the good in others with a new sense of compassion, and you will move beyond fear into freedom.

Are you ready to face the facts? Then let's do it!

CHAPTER 9

THE SOUL-MATH™ FORMULA

Facts do not cease to exist because they are ignored.
—Aldous Huxley

BEFORE EXPLAINING THE Soul-Math Formula and how it works, it's important for you to understand *why* it works. The formula is based upon the concept that our thoughts, feelings, and beliefs will influence our actions, and the combination of these four factors will produce the results we refer to as experiences, circumstances, challenges, problems, or blessings. The results are specific to the relationship between these factors. Here's the formula:

Thought x Feeling x Belief x Action = Experience/Result

Power of Will

Now let me warn you about one very important thing. We all know that everything begins as a thought. Many people believe that "thoughts are things," or declare, "If you change your thinking, you can change your life!" This is true but incomplete. Your emotions, or feelings, play an extremely important part in this equation. Typically, we have between fifty thousand and seventy thousand thoughts per day. That's between thirty-five and forty-eight thoughts per minute! To say that every one of those thoughts will affect your life is not reasonable. But here's my point: *only the thoughts fueled by a congruent feeling have power.*

Did you get that? It's powerful. Here's another real shocker. If a thought and a feeling support each other, and are repeated in your consciousness long enough, *they become a belief!* That's when your subconscious belief system takes over and literally controls the thoughts and feelings that you will take seriously, or even allow yourself to consider. This means that the power of your thoughts and feelings are greatly reduced and even constructive thoughts and feelings may be rejected because your belief system doesn't support them.

This is one reason why The Soul-Math Formula is so effective and life-changing. Our belief system, which I often refer to as our BS, is usually a deep, long-standing, buried but powerful control system governing how we manage and create our experiences of life. Soul-Math will assist you in analyzing your creative factors and reveal beliefs that just may astonish you! Then you will see what has to be changed and/or forgiven. Don't worry. I'll help you figure out how to make those changes. But first, let's make sure you thoroughly understand the formula. Once you get the hang of it, you'll find it very rewarding. In fact, I predict you'll use it often.

Understanding The Soul-Math™ Formula and Its Factors

This amazing formula is made up of the primary factors behind every result you have been getting in your life. It's all about zeroing in on a challenge, situation, concern, or fear you may be facing and analyzing the factors contributing to it. What you reveal will help you understand why that issue exists for you or why you perceive it as problematic.

If you are searching for answers to more than one circumstance, work through them one at a time. You may be surprised at how the answers you reveal having to do with one issue might overlap others and make the discovery of solutions to several problems much easier. It's vitally important to understand that if you have hit a wall with respect to some problem in your life, even if you didn't personally create it, something in your own consciousness may be getting in the way of resolving the problem or managing it in a new and effective way. Be honest with your answers as you fill out a worksheet, and don't let the problem overpower your intention to resolve it, rise above it, and take command of your own experience!

I just used the word *consciousness*, and I want to clarify my personal definition of that word. The dictionary definition of consciousness ranges from "being awake and aware of one's surroundings" to "awareness by the mind of itself and the world." My use of that word isn't in conflict with these definitions, simply more specific. When I use the word *consciousness*, I am referring to the combination or sum total of one's thoughts, feelings, and beliefs. In other words, the key components of The Soul-Math Formula! Your consciousness directs your actions and determines or influences the results you experience.

Keep in mind that the equation becomes more complex as you study each component and as you take an honest, in-depth look at the ways in which the various factors affect one another. Here is an illustration of the formula describing each factor so that you start out with a clear understanding.

Understanding the Soul-Math™ Formula

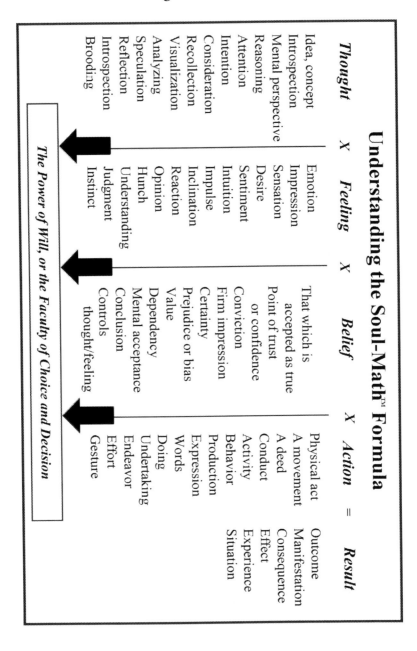

Thought	x	*Feeling*	x	*Belief*	x	*Action*	=	*Result*
Idea, concept		Emotion		That which is accepted as true		Physical act		Outcome
Introspection		Impression		Point of trust or confidence		A movement		Manifestation
Mental perspective		Sensation		Conviction		A deed		Consequence
Reasoning		Desire		Firm impression		Conduct		Effect
Attention		Sentiment		Certainty		Activity		Experience
Intention		Intuition		Prejudice or bias		Behavior		Situation
Consideration		Impulse		Value		Production		
Recollection		Inclination		Dependency		Expression		
Visualization		Reaction		Mental acceptance		Words		
Analyzing		Opinion		Conclusion		Doing		
Speculation		Hunch		Controls thought/feeling		Undertaking		
Reflection		Understanding				Endeavor		
Introspection		Judgment				Effort		
Brooding		Instinct				Gesture		

The Power of Will, or the Faculty of Choice and Decision

Now let's take a closer look at how the factors affect and interact with one another to produce various results. Suppose you have a *thought* about some problem or concern, and you have a congruent or harmonizing *feeling* about that same thing. Okay, the thought and feeling are in agreement. But what if one or more of your *beliefs* are opposed to the thought/feeling combo? Well, here's what happens: the contrary *belief* will throw up a mental block and you will take no new action that could change the result you've been getting.

For instance, let's say you've fallen in love. Your *thought* might be "I want to marry this person." Your *feeling* nature agrees: "Yes, because I feel great love for this person." But rooted in your *belief system* is your perception "I'm afraid of commitment." This deep-seated and hypnotic belief will override your thought and feeling. As a result, you make no wedding plans.

The equation now looks like this:

Thought x Feeling   x Belief   x~~Action~~ = Nothing New
    (Congruent)   (Incongruent)

The above equation has become a formula for daydreaming or fantasizing, not a formula for creating something new or for moving forward.

Now let's say you entertain a *thought* about something; a career choice, for instance. Your logical *thought* might be "I'm really good at math, biology, and calculus, so I should become a scientist." But your *feelings* are saying, "I hate science, but I would love to be an artist!" Your *belief* system in the meantime might have rooted within it the idea "Artists make no money." So you decide to act on your *thoughts* controlled by your *belief,* and you decide to become a scientist. But you are miserable, or at least unfulfilled, because you're not motivated by your *feeling* nature. The equation would now look like this:

Thought x~~Feeling~~ x Belief x Action =
Short-lived or Forced Result

Now the equation has become a formula for *temporary results,* or *forced outcome.* It lacks the congruent *feeling* that is the motivator or the yeast that makes the bread rise. The only way the outcome of this equation could last very long would be through sheer willpower and a process of struggle, striving, and force. There are many people living such lives of unhappiness and unfulfilled desire.

Yet another possibility is to ignore your thoughts and beliefs and just go with the *feelings* about something. Take for instance being on a date with someone who proposes having sex. Your *emotions* are crying out, "Yes, go for it!" But your *thoughts* are countering with "I won't think much of myself in the morning," backed by the belief "Sex without love makes me no better than a prostitute." But you get carried away with the emotional surge and take action anyway. The result is you don't think much of yourself in the morning, and you further reinforce the *belief* that you're no better than a prostitute. The equation would now look like this:

**~~Thought x~~ Feeling ~~x Belief~~ x Action =
Disappointing or Regretful Result**

The equation now becomes a formula for emotion-backed reactions that override the balancing factor of mental clarity and belief. It becomes the formula for addictive, impulsive behavior. This is clearly not the path to peace and balance.

The point is, none of these combinations will create a happy, healthy, reliable outcome or result because some of the factors are not in agreement with each other. And all factors must agree!

Now let's look at what the times sign (x) between the factors represent. They represent your *power of will* that joins the factors together. Your power of will is the power of *choice* and *decision*. Your power of will makes it possible for you to keep the factors in alignment. Only when all factors are in agreement will you get a result that is consistent with the intent. For example, in order for a result to be positive, all factors must be positive. The congruent positive equation would look like this:

**_Positive_ Thought x _Positive_ Feeling x _Positive_ Belief
x _Positive_ Action = _Positive_ Result**

But keep in mind that the creative process works both ways. In other words, *negative congruency* will produce *negative results*. The *congruent negative* equation would look like this:

Negative **Thought x** **Negative** **Feeling x** **Negative** **Belief**
x **Negative** **Action =** **Negative** **Result**

An incongruent equation, or an equation that mixes positive factors with negative factors, will bring about results that are confusing, immobilizing, and unreliable, thus producing outcomes that will look like mistakes.

The Power of Choice and Decision as the Function of Your Will

Decision is a sharp knife that cuts clean and straight; indecision, a dull one that hacks and tears and leaves ragged edges behind it.
—Gordon Graham

As I mentioned, the times sign (x) between each of the Soul-Math factors represents the *power of will* and is the glue that holds the factors in place. Your will is perhaps the most important and powerful faculty with which you've been gifted. It is your power of will that multiplies the effectiveness of these factors when congruent with one another.

Now when I say power of will, I'm not talking about willpower, or the ability to manipulate. I'm referring to your wise or unwise use of choice and decision. Your power of will acts as a behind-the-scenes director, or energy manager, that controls and guides your personal creative factors of thought, feeling, belief, and action. The main function of this "director" is to use choice and decision to determine the quality of these factors. This director is what shapes The Soul-Math Formula into a kind of mathematical equation.

Every move you make, every thought you think, every word you speak, every feeling you have, and every action you take involves *choosing*, either consciously or unconsciously. Even when you think you are sitting in indecision, you have chosen not to choose!

You might be wondering if there's a difference between choice and decision. There are many debates about that, but here's my take on it. Yes, there's a difference, although choice and decision work together. In simple terms, I believe choice to be a matter of selection. But when you select something, it doesn't mean you will act upon that selection until you make a firm decision. For instance, let's say there's a person in your life you have *chosen* to love, but you can't *decide* whether or not to marry that person. That's a big difference!

Here's another example: Imagine making plans to attend an upscale event where everyone will be dressed to the hilt. You think to yourself, *I better go out and buy a new outfit!* You then bring to mind what type of outfit you'd like to wear on that occasion. So you go to a top-notch store and stand in the main aisle by the appropriate clothing department, scanning all the racks of clothes at a distance. Then you spot it! There it is, way across the room, hanging on a rack. Exactly what you had in mind! You consciously *choose* that item. But if you keep standing there just staring at it from a distance and make no move to go over to the rack, take it into a fitting room to try it on, and then take it to the checkout counter to pay for it and leave the store with it, you haven't *decided* to take the action that makes you the owner of your choice. So my thinking is that decisions are about owning your choices.

Decision is one of the most powerful tools you have because decision declares *intention*. That's why it's so important that you learn how to create a healthy mind that will stop making erroneous, unconscious decisions. You must learn to begin making wise decisions at a conscious level— decisions that you are prepared to act upon with unwavering confidence.

People often come to me in a state of confusion and unhappiness because they think they can't decide what to do. It doesn't take long, as the observer, to see that they *have* made a decision at an unconscious level. But because their thoughts, polluted with judgment and unhappy images, are pulling them in one direction—and their heart, bogged down with sticky, heavy emotions is pulling them in another, they're rendered incapable of making an intelligent, conscious decision. As a result, they walk around in a state of total confusion. Remember the Soul-Math rules: to get a positive result, you must have your thoughts, feelings, beliefs, and actions in harmonious, positive alignment.

One woman came to me in great distress because she hated her job and things seemed to be deteriorating at the office. She said her boss was verbally abusive and inconsiderate, there was trouble with coworkers and their lack of cooperation, her work was boring, and she was overworked. The list went on and on.

"What do you *desire*?" I asked.

She gave me a blank stare. "I don't know" was her reply.

"Have you considered that you can't move out of an unpleasant situation if you don't know what it is you desire?" I asked.

Another blank stare.

Then I asked her, "Have you, at some level, *decided* that your *desire* is to leave your present job?"

"Yes," she replied after a long hesitation.

"Now we're getting somewhere," I said. "Decision moves us forward."

From that point on, I was able to help this woman see that she wasn't unclear or indecisive at all, but that she simply hadn't recognized her desire or decision at a conscious level. This awareness enabled her to look at that decision in light of the diagnostic worksheet she had filled out. She could see how all her fearful thoughts and negative feelings, as well as her limiting beliefs, had kept her from bringing her decision to conscious awareness.

This woman had stayed in her job out of fear, not realizing that she had already made an unconscious decision in favor of leaving. Her fears included the following:

- What if I don't find another job right away?
- How will I support myself?
- What if I can't get another job with the same salary?

Her fearful mind-chatter produced contradictory head-thoughts and fearful heart-thoughts. A battle raged within her. She began to create situations that would justify her feelings and eventually *force* her out of the job. This way, she wouldn't have to make a *conscious* decision. Her relationship with coworkers started to deteriorate. She began experiencing physical symptoms as she got ready for work each morning. She was cross and irritable. She began making mistakes. Before long, it seemed as though everything was working against her. She was able to say to herself, "See? I told you this was a rotten job and my boss is a tyrant!"

By the time she came to see me, she was miserable. I explained that if she kept doing what she was doing, she would keep getting what she was getting. Her life would become so unhappy that she would get laid off, fired, or quit in a snit. Then she could say, "I just couldn't stand it anymore!" One way or another, she would get what she *really* desired, which was to leave the job. The decision would finally win out, but because she was fighting against it, it would manifest through struggle.

The correct approach in a situation like this is to acknowledge the decision, bring it up to a conscious level, and look at it head-on. This means laying aside all fear and having enough confidence to create a plan to carry out the decision.

Once this woman clearly saw that her decision was rooted in fear, she was in a position to review her choices. She could honor her decision, release all fearful thoughts, and put a conscious plan into motion so she could gracefully and happily leave the job. Or she could decide to keep her job and embrace it with a new attitude of creative enthusiasm. She could *decide* to be happy staying where she was until her next steps unfolded naturally.

What is your state of mind when you are *indecisive?* Worry. Indecision is always accompanied by worry. If you feel you can't make a decision, you are in a state of worry about making the wrong decision. Worry is mental impotency. It's a vicious circle. When you worry, you can't make a decision, or if you try to make a decision while worrying, you just worry more. Worries are useless mental gymnastics that do nothing but retard progress. Worry limits your choices and leads to indecision. Indecision is the decision to fail. Failure not only means no forward movement but mental, emotional, physical, and spiritual degeneration. What is the soul doing while all this is happening? It just sits there—waiting—hidden by all the unintelligent rubbish. It's like a valuable bar of gold that has been painted with black paint and buried in the dirt, disguised as a piece of iron. It feels heavy, burdened, and very, very black. But underneath is still a gold bar, waiting to be unveiled.

A decision is a resting place for your mind. As you move forward, each decision provides you with a stopping place, a place of relief, a place of peace. Each decision is the completion of a movement of thought. When you reach a decision, you stop all possibility of worry for the present moment in the present situation.

The most common reason for having difficulty making conscious, confident decisions is the fear of making a mistake. There are three steps out of this dilemma. Take these following steps and you'll successfully apply your power of will:

1. Stop worrying about making a mistake.
2. Choose with a sense of childlike innocence and confidence.
3. Accept your decision and own your choice with a sense of peace.

Now, if you're ready, we'll move on to actually working The Soul-Math Formula.

CHAPTER 10

THE SOUL-MATH™ FORMULA:
ANALYZING THE PROBLEM

It requires a very unusual mind to undertake the analysis of the obvious.
—Alfred North Whitehead

WORKING WITH THE Soul-Math Formula is like taking part in an archeological dig. With a little effort and patience, you will unearth whatever is buried deep within your consciousness that has brought you to this point in time. Once you find the interferences, you can take steps to change things.

The Soul-Math Formula is also a great tool to diagnose and reveal the areas of your consciousness that are preventing you from making important decisions. It will point out where the blocks are, what's holding you hostage, and what's keeping you from reaching a decision. It may even point out a subconscious decision you didn't realize you had made. You could do a worksheet on the subject of your indecisiveness. In fact, you can do a worksheet on just about anything!

On the next page, you'll find a blank diagnostic worksheet, followed by a step-by-step explanation of how to use it, along with Joe's example. Chapter Eleven will explain the correction worksheet and how Joe completed his. In Chapter Twelve, you'll find two more examples of how people used both the diagnostic and correction worksheets to help them change their lives. In addition to Joe's example, there's Carol's story and an amazing testimonial by Mackenzie that I feel certain will inspire you. Their worksheets are also included.

Diagnostic Worksheet

The Soul-Math™ Formula
Diagnostic Worksheet

1. Existing circumstance needing correction: —————— **Date:** ——

Thought x	Feeling x	Belief x	Action =	Present Situation
3. Record your typical thoughts as they relate to #1.	4. Record your typical emotions and feelings as they relate to #1.	5. What do you believe as related to #1? Dig Deep!	6. Record current patterns of action and behavior.	2. How are things now? What is the result you are experiencing?

Using the Diagnostic Worksheet

Step 1: What circumstance needs correcting?

This is a simple statement about the situation you want to change or the problem you're facing and should be recorded on the top line. Do not make it a question. If there is more than one situation in your life that needs attention, pick one. It's easier to handle one thing at a time. Besides, you may find after doing this that some of the other problems in your life will also improve or change.

Step 2: How are things now?

In the far-right column labeled "Present Situation", make a list that describes in detail what's going in your life as a result of the problem stated in Step One. This should be results or conditions, not random thoughts or feelings. Examples might be "I'm stuck. I'm physically worn out. I'm grumpy most of the time." Making this list is like stepping back, becoming the observer, and realizing how many areas of your life are adversely affected by this unresolved circumstance or problem.

Step 3: What are your thoughts?

In the "Thought" column on the far left, write down what you've been thinking about the situation recorded at the top of your worksheet. This may be a mix of negative and positive thoughts, whatever comes up. And don't worry if what comes to mind is more of a feeling or an emotion than a thought or even a belief. There's a place for those too. Just write them down in the appropriate column and keep going.

Step 4: What are your feelings?

In the "Feeling" column, record your feelings and emotions about the problem. If you come up with something that seems more like a thought, go back and put it in the "Thought" column. Don't worry about getting something in the wrong column. What's important is that you're delving deep inside your mind and heart. You may be surprised at how much precious time has been spent dwelling on thoughts and feelings related to this problem.

Step 5: What are your beliefs?

As you dig deeper and deeper into your psyche, hidden beliefs will jump out and sometimes shock you as you realize what's been behind all those thoughts and feelings. Put these in the "Belief" column. Be sure to list obvious beliefs you already know have influenced your thoughts and feelings. These could be religious beliefs or beliefs taught you by parents or past experiences.

Step 6: What actions have you taken?

The "Action" column is where you record what you *do* with much of your time. This list will speak volumes about what you've been *doing* or *not doing* with respect to the problem you're analyzing. If the other columns are full of negatives, you may find the "Action" column to be almost void of any constructive actions. As a side note, your "Action" column will tell you a lot about your hidden beliefs!

Keep This in Mind …

As I've already mentioned, don't be overly concerned about getting the right words in the right columns. Sometimes it's hard to tell whether an impulse is a thought, a feeling, or a belief. Just put it where it feels right. You might even want to put it in all three columns. Just stay with the process, and eventually you'll see what needs to change to produce a new result.

Also, I hope as you fill out a worksheet that you realize the powerful ways you've been using your thoughts, feelings, beliefs, and actions to create your present situation. Notice the struggle you've been experiencing because of them. Then, when you think you've gone as far as you can with your worksheet, lay it aside. Believe me, more information will surface. When it does, go back and add it. You may even consider carrying your worksheet, or at least a small notebook, with you so when something new arises, you can write it down. And please be patient. Completing your worksheet may take several days, but it will be well worth it.

A word of warning here: you may hit a wall and feel like abandoning the process. If so, know that it's because you're used to living in a comfort zone of addictive patterns that generate fear when on the verge of a breakthrough. Keep going! Use your power of decision to expand your comfort zone!

In the Soul-Math classes I teach, everyone who devotes adequate time to doing the worksheets and really digging into themselves has found how involved, fascinating, explosive, and intricate the process can become. The insights that occur are invaluable. As your emotions and beliefs surface, the puzzle starts to come together.

Before beginning your own process, take some time to study the following examples accompanied by sample diagnostic and corrective worksheets. The first one has to do with Joe.

Joe's Diagnostic Worksheet

Joe came to me feeling angry, anxious, and stuck about what to do next. He was very dissatisfied with his job, and his disenchantment was affecting his home life, friendships, and overall happiness. After some discussion about how he could discover what to do about his dilemma, he agreed to work through the Soul-Math process. Here's how we walked through the steps of the diagnostic process, along with a copy of Joe's completed worksheet.

Step 1: What circumstance needs correcting?

Joe's *existing circumstance* is "I'm really unhappy with my job." As you will see, even though he's focused upon his job, every area of his life is being affected.

Step 2: How are things now?

Here Joe listed the *way things are*, the facts as he presently sees them. Notice how his attitude toward his job has affected other areas of his life as well, including his health and relationships.

Step 3: Joe's thoughts

Notice that Joe's thoughts are all negative. When you do your own worksheet, you may have some positive thoughts as well. But in Joe's case, he has a lot of correction to do!

Step 4: Joe's feelings

As you can see, Joe did an honest evaluation of his feelings and emotions. And once again, his feelings are mostly negative. But your worksheet may contain some positive feelings as well.

Step 5: Joe's beliefs

Here's where the rubber meets the road. After analyzing his conscious beliefs relating to his job, Joe's hidden beliefs began to surface. If you do the work, yours will too. To get there, ask yourself, "What are my underlying beliefs about this situation, about myself, about my religious perspective, about others, about anything and everything?" Like Joe, if you answer honestly, you will uncover deep-seated beliefs that must be changed if you want to turn things around. Sometimes making this change will be as easy as saying, "I don't really believe that!" or "I no longer believe that!" But sometimes it takes a little more work to transform that negative, worn-out, or false belief into a fresh, new understanding that supports the changes you want to make.

Step 6: Joe's actions

Notice that Joe's current actions look more like no action or destructive action rather than positive forward movement. They also go beyond those behavior patterns directly related to his job dilemma. This clearly shows how Joe's thoughts, feelings, and beliefs about his job have affected other areas of his life. The same thing will hold true for you.

For several days, Joe kept having new revelations about his situation. As a result, he went back many times to add to his worksheet. Eventually, he held in his hands an honest evaluation of his consciousness.

It doesn't take a rocket scientist to figure out that Joe had a lot of work to do. But even though he felt somewhat discouraged, he was determined to make changes in his life. He reached out for counseling to help him create a new game plan.

Joe's Diagnostic Worksheet

The Soul-Math™ Formula
Joe's Diagnostic Worksheet

Sample Worksheet

1. Existing circumstance needing correction: ____ *I'm really unhappy with my job.* ____ **Date:** ____

3. Record your typical thoughts as they relate to #1.	4. Record your typical emotions and feelings as they relate to #1.	5. What do you believe as related to #1? Dig Deep!	6. Record current patterns of action and behavior.	2. How are things now? What is the result you are experiencing?
Thought x	**Feeling** x	**Belief** x	**Action** =	**Present Situation**
My boss doesn't like me. This job is boring. I'm overworked. I'm not paid enough. If I change jobs, maybe I won't like it any better. I'll make the best of it. I hope no one else gets a raise either. Somebody else always gets the credit. What if I lose my job? I never have any fun. Who would want to read my resume? I couldn't face the idea of interviewing for a job.	The world's against me. I'm angry. I'm afraid to quit. I feel inadequate. There's no other choice. (futility, hopelessness) I'm sad. (despair) I feel guilty for not doing my best. I'm frustrated. I'm so unhappy. Life sucks. (depression) Why try? (self-pity) I'm unappreciated. I can't stand him/her! I'm useless. I was born to fail. I'm not good enough. I'll never forgive him/her	My job is my source. (God is not my source) It's someone else's fault. I'm not worth having a job I like and enjoy. God doesn't support me. I can't trust life. People can't be trusted. (God can't be trusted either) Life is a struggle. I'm a victim. I am powerless. I'm worthless. I'm useless. I was born to fail. I'm not good enough.	Lethary Immobilization Retelling my story over and over and over. Focusing on what it is I don't want. Critical judgment of boss, co-workers, etc. Sitting too much (no exercise) Overeating	I hate my job. My body is showing signs of ill-health. My life is out of balance. My body is unfit. My family ignores me. I didn't get a raise. I'm stuck in a job I hate.

My Review of Joe's Diagnostic Worksheet

1. Look at the Action column. Notice how Joe's thoughts, feelings, and beliefs have paralyzed him. When there is no positive action, nothing can change for the better. But his actions aren't likely to change without first changing the other factors.

2. Notice that it takes a great deal of honest introspection to admit that you have negative beliefs about yourself and especially about God. Joe had to admit that if he felt afraid to quit his job, he was seeing the job as his source instead of God as his Source. So beware of saying, "I believe in God," when what you may actually believe in is your own fear-based thoughts and feelings as the power in your life. If you truly believe in God, there can be no fear; there is only faith.

3. On Joe's worksheet, the thoughts, feelings, and beliefs are congruent and in agreement with one another. They're all negative. Therefore, his actions are fairly negative and self-destructive. When *you* do a worksheet, you too may find that your thoughts and feelings about a particular idea are congruently negative. But at the same time, you may think that your belief about that idea is positive. Go back and be even more honest with yourself. There's something you're not seeing. More than likely your *belief* isn't as positive as you first thought.

4. Notice that Joe's particular equation adds up to stagnation. An attempt, however, to change just *some* thoughts, feelings, and beliefs will open the door for new action that is constructive and expansive instead of limiting and constricting.

Further Comments on the Diagnostic Worksheet

Over the past several years, I've used The Soul-Math Formula during many of my counseling sessions to help people see where their hidden problems lie. After filling out the diagnostic worksheet, they realize that what they thought was their problem is not the real problem at all! It's just a surface symptom. So use the worksheet to dig deep. Peel away the layers of the onion, and get rid of all the surface excuses and smoke screens. When you're finished, you will hold in your hands a written copy of your present state of consciousness. This is where the real core issues are, what your thoughts, feelings, beliefs, and actions have kept buried for so long. Now you can start to make improvements in your life.

One final thought before we move on. Never let your worksheet overwhelm you so that you become discouraged about the consciousness work you have to do. Your objective is to be a happy, fulfilled person. So take one step at a time, acknowledge yourself for the work you're doing, and enjoy the process.

CHAPTER 11

THE SOUL-MATH™ FORMULA: TURNING THINGS AROUND

The beginning is the most important part of the work.
—Plato

Making Consciousness U-turns

BY COMPLETING YOUR diagnostic worksheet honestly and with clear intention, the hard work is over! Now comes the real fun— turning things around! Now I know what you're thinking. *Fun?! You think this has been fun?! This hasn't exactly been a walk in the park for me!*

Okay, maybe not. I admit the diagnostic phase can be a bit uncomfortable, especially if your worksheet is as negative as Joe's. But think about it. You've taken a hard look at those things you've been ignoring for a long time, perhaps many years. Either that or you've uncovered things you didn't even know were there. And come on, don't you feel the least bit better just knowing what the real problems are? Now you can do something about them!

The correction phase of The Soul-Math Formula helps you create a map of what I call "consciousness U-turns." These are changes you absolutely must make to get the result you want.

As you consider what you've written in all the columns of your diagnostic worksheet, I imagine you're already beginning to see a new action plan forming, one sure to produce positive results. And believe me, that plan will guide you in ways you never dreamed possible.

One last thing before we get into the correction worksheet: once completed, you may feel a bit overwhelmed. It may be you simply aren't ready to make some of the U-turns on the list. You may even refuse to make some of them. That's okay. Just go through the worksheet and circle the changes you feel comfortable making. Let the other stuff go for now. I've learned that when people start by making changes they feel ready to make, many of the other things take care of themselves. Either that or they become less threatening or impossible. So don't worry.

Now let's take a look at the Soul-Math correction worksheet, and then see how Joe did his.

Correction Worksheet

The Soul-Math™ Formula
Correction Worksheet

Date: _____

1. **Existing circumstance needing correction:** _____

3. Record highest possible thoughts that would be in support of #2.	4. Record highest possible emotions that would be in support of #2.	5. Record highest possible beliefs in support of #2.	6. What would patterns of action be in support of #2?	2. State desired result.
Thought x	**Feeling** x	**Belief** x	**Action** =	**Result**

Joe's Correction Worksheet

After analyzing his situation with me, Joe took his worksheets home and did some soul-searching in private. Then he came back, and we discussed the changes he needed to make to turn things around. I could already see some of those changes taking place in him simply as a result of his willingness to take a new look at himself. His anger was less intense, his attitude was softening, and he seemed ready to set a new plan into motion. Here's an outline of how Joe approached the correction process followed by his actual worksheet.

Step 1: What circumstance needs correcting?

Joe's *existing circumstance* is still "I'm unhappy with my job." But as you'll soon see, he's about to make some bold positive statements to change that.

Step 2: How would I like things to be?

Now Joe is getting real. Here he's listed what he really wants. It's no-holds-barred!

Steps 3–5: Joe's thoughts, feelings, and beliefs

Joe has converted every negative thought, feeling, and belief statement on his diagnostic worksheet into a positive opposite. Now he can start to see what action steps he needs to take to make his dreams a reality.

Step 6: Joe's actions

By comparing his diagnostic worksheet to his correction worksheet, Joe has created his map of consciousness U-turns along with the actions he must take to get the results he wants.

Joe's Correction Worksheet

Sample Worksheet

The Soul-Math™ Formula
Joe's Correction Worksheet

Date: _____

1. Existing circumstance needing correction: *I'm unhappy with my job.*

3. Record your highest thoughts that would be in support of #2.	4. Record your highest emotions that would be in support of #2.	5. Record your highest beliefs that would be in support of #2.	6. What would patterns of action be like in support of #2?	2. State desired result.
Thought x	**Feeling** x	**Belief** x	**Action** =	**Present Situation**
My boss is responding to me in a positive way.	I feel loved.	With God all things are possible.	I am ready to take action!	I am happy with my present job and open to the next perfect position!
I love my present job without thinking I have to stay forever.	I still want a new job, but I am happy NOW.	I take responsibility.	Stop telling my sad story.	It provides me with the income I desire, chance for promotion, private office, lots of light, pleasant people, etc.
I love expressing myself in my present job.	I trust God to support me.	I am worth having a job I like and enjoy.	I am focused on what it is that I want for my life.	My life is balanced.
This job experience has taught me so much!	I feel capable.	I trust God – I trust life.	Daily choice to be happy.	My relationships are happier.
I choose to be happy.	I feel inspired!	Everyone is my teacher.	I stop all critical judgment.	I am fulfilled.
I want the highest for everyone around me.	I am enthusiastic about life – and this job!	Life is easy!	Daily exercise and healthy choices.	I am successful.
I am acknowledged for my input.	I am doing my best!	I am a success!	Prepare resume.	I enjoy using my talents and creativity.
My resume is attracting the perfect job for me.	I feel calm and peaceful.	I am powerful!	Conduct job search.	Life is Good!
	I feel forgiving.	I am an important part of the whole of life.	Do necessary skill-building	
	I accept everyone just the way they are.	I am capable.	Contact someone to coach my interview skills.	
	I accept myself just the way I am.	I am good enough!	Meditate daily.	
	I accept other people.	All things work together for good.	Create a clear vision.	
	I forgive everyone.		Do something for others.	
			Say affirmations daily.	

CHAPTER 12

TWO MORE AMAZING SUCCESS STORIES

Setting an example is not the main means of
influencing another, it is the only means.
—Albert Einstein

THE SOUL-MATH FORMULA helped Joe see how changing his consciousness could change his experience. It took a lot of sincere and heartfelt work, but he managed to transform much of his unhappiness into success and satisfaction. He did finally leave his job, but he did so amiably. What's more, he not only received a letter of recommendation, but he stays in touch with many of his former coworkers he now considers his friends.

Joe is a good example of how things can turn around after using The Soul-Math Formula. Now I'd like to share Carol's amazing story.

Carol's Story: A Failing Marriage

When Carol came into my office, her marriage was falling apart. She described her relationship with her husband, Sam, as "uninteresting, boring, and humdrum."

"He's never amounted to anything, and we never have any money," she added. She then went on to describe their shabby surroundings, blaming Sam for never doing anything to fix up the house. "He only wants to come home from work, have a drink, eat dinner, and park himself on the sofa to watch television," she ranted.   Her complaints went on and on. Finally, she ran out of steam. She looked up at me and painfully asked, "What can I do?"

There was nothing Carol could do to change Sam. But I knew if I could get her to move her focus beyond what she perceived to be Sam's shortcomings to how she might be contributing to her own misery, it would make a big difference in her life, perhaps both of their lives. So I introduced her to The Soul-Math Formula, and we started filling in the blanks on a diagnostic worksheet.

Carol's Diagnostic Worksheet

To begin with, Carol's Thought and Feeling columns were very negative. So I asked her, "Aren't there any *positive* thoughts to add to the equation?" At first, she didn't want to admit that some things Sam did were, in fact, positive influences on their marriage. Then she became quiet and thoughtful. After a few minutes, she wiped tears from her eyes and began recounting the good things.

Sam, she said, was loyal and supportive of her and her own pursuits. He hadn't missed a day of work in years, and whenever she wanted to go somewhere, he generally agreed. He didn't argue with or yell at her and never abused her in any way. He had a good relationship with their grown children. What's more, she said, Sam was handsome, dependable, and consistent.

As she scribbled these things down on her worksheet, it occurred to me that many women would think Sam was the perfect husband. Carol, however, was too wrapped up in her own state of disenchantment and poor Sam was taking the blame.

Next, Carol started on the Feelings column. This time, she not only listed negative feelings about her husband but also about herself. I finally asked Carol if she had any *positive feelings* she could add. After thinking a bit, she answered, "I love Sam deep down." That was all she could come up with at the time. If there was more, it was so buried in her current emotional state that only her unhappiness was evident. It was apparent that before we could shift her perspective and get her to look at her husband as well as herself with new eyes, we needed to get her off the pity pot.

Moving on to the Belief column, Carol was in for a real shock. All her life she had professed a belief in God and claimed that God was Love. But after a lot of soul-searching and honesty, she had to admit that her belief at a deeper level didn't add up to someone who really believed in God's love. In fact, if she believed at all, it was in a judgmental God who plays favorites. And as if that wasn't enough, Carol realized that she didn't believe in herself.

Finally, we came to the Action column. I asked Carol, "When Sam is doing what he typically does, what are you doing?" It was just as I had suspected. She did the same thing he did! She had a drink with him, served dinner, and then watched TV, brooding the whole time and becoming more unhappy and resentful.

Obviously, Carol needed to make some changes. She had to break her routine and do something new and different. She had to stop expecting Sam to meet her demands and do something to please herself. But most importantly, she had to *decide* to change her attitude and begin thinking and acting out the *positive opposite* of what she'd been doing.

Carol's Diagnostic Worksheet

Sample Worksheet

The Soul-Math™ Formula
Carol's Diagnostic Worksheet

Date: _____

1. Existing circumstance needing correction: ___ *I'm unhappily married.* ___

3. Record your typical thoughts as they relate to #1.	4. Record your typical emotions and feelings as they relate to #1.	5. What do you believe as related to #1? Dig Deep!	6. Record current patterns of action and behavior.	2. How are things now? What is the result you are experiencing?
Thought x	**Feeling** x	**Belief** x	**Action** =	**Present Situation**
(Carol's answers at first) My marriage is boring. Sam is a lazy failure. It's all Sam's fault. I can't make it on my own. I'm stuck in this marriage. Sam's let this house go to pot. We never do anything fun. *(Answers when asked about positives)* Sam is a loyal husband. He's supportive. He's usually patient. He's a good father. He never misses work. He doesn't argue. He goes where I want to go. He's handsome. He's dependable/consistent.	I'm angry with Sam. I feel resentful. I'm angry with myself. I feel helpless. Useless. I feel angry when a friend gets something new. I feel embarrassed. I'm unhappy and sad. I feel depressed a lot. I feel worthless. I feel used. I feel unfulfilled. I feel inadequate. I feel like I'm being punished. *(Answer when asked about positive feelings)* I love Sam deep down.	I believe in God. But I guess I don't believe God loves me. I say I have faith but I don't believe God can help me. I guess I really believe that God is a judgmental God playing favorites. I don't believe in myself. I believe that I'm stuck in lack and limitation. Life is a struggle. I believe in the luck of the draw (Whatever comes down the pike). I can't do anything on my own.	I do what Sam does. When he gets home, I have a drink with him. I serve dinner I watch TV. I brood all evening and add to the anger and resentment. I do nothing. I talk about my sad story a lot to friends/family.	My marriage is failing.

Carol's Correction Worksheet

I sent Carol home with instructions for doing the correction worksheet. She faithfully complied, adding to it every day. Following several additional meetings with me, Carol became clear that her unhappiness had nothing to do with Sam. It was about her and her attitude. She decided to start making some changes.

The next time I saw her, her smile was bright and she walked with a lighter step. She told me that instead of waiting for Sam to do something, she'd taken the initiative herself and was sprucing up their home without spending a lot of money. She'd even begun cleaning out closets and giving things away she hadn't used in years. Even Sam was getting into the act. Before she knew it, they were painting the bedroom together.

Glowing with success, Carol was now ready to look at even more new positive possibilities. We discussed her talents and what she felt confident doing. She had a history in local theater and loved to sing and dance. She loved to work with kids. Her renewed enthusiasm eventually led her to the perfect job, creating educational programs for children. Not only that, she suddenly found herself with enough income and money to spare.

I saw Carol one more time professionally. What Sam did or did not do was less important to her now. She was learning to accept him just as he was and to move herself into positive action doing all the things that made her happy. Sometime later, my husband and I ran into Carol and Sam at the theater. There was this smiling, handsome couple enjoying each other. You'd never know their marriage had once been close to ending.

I didn't see Carol again until five years later. She walked into my office just to say hello. The happy, bubbly, successful woman who stood before me bore absolutely no resemblance to the defeated complainer I met years earlier. She told me she and Sam were doing all kinds of wonderful things together. What's more, she was supervising a music and dance program for hundreds of children, with eight teachers under her direction.

Carol is an example of what can happen if someone is willing to do the work and make necessary changes in their life. When she turned her thoughts and feelings around, started thinking of ways to express her natural gifts, and focused on ways to give rather than get, things really began to take off. And it can happen for you too.

Carol's Correction Worksheet

Sample
Worksheet

The Soul-Math™ Formula
Carol's Correction Worksheet

Date: _____

1. **Existing circumstance needing correction:** _I'm unhappily married_

3. Record your highest thoughts that would be in support of #2.		4. Record your highest emotions that would be in support of #2.		5. Record your highest beliefs that would be in support of #2.		6. What would patterns of action be like in support of #2?		2. State desired result.
Thought	x	**Feeling**	x	**Belief**	x	**Action**	=	**Present Situation**
I am free to be me. My marriage is as alive as I am. I can love my house, regardless of Sam's feelings. I appreciate Sam's loyalty. I appreciate his attitude and his dependability. Sam has taught me many lessons. I'm not stuck in marriage. I'm stuck in my own perception. I can recreate everything. I respect and honor Sam. I accept Sam as he is. I acknowledge my soul.		I am grateful for Sam! I forgive him. I forgive myself. I am never helpless. I rejoice in other people's good fortune. I am enthusiastic! I am love! I feel inspired and creative. I accept everyone just the way they are. I accept myself just the way I am. I love using my talents. I feel appreciated. My soul feels nurtured.		I believe in myself! I deserve to be happy. I am free to make my own choices and decisions. Life is easy! I create my own reality. I rely on God as my Source. I have renewed faith.		I choose to have a cup of tea with Sam instead of an alcoholic beverage. Be pleasant and interested in Sam during dinner. Listen to him. After dinner I will start on my projects for the children's program. Write out a plan of action to express my musical and teaching talents. Research ideas to spruce up the house at a low cost.		I am vitally alive, creative, productive, and happily married.

Mackenzie's Story: A Struggling Business

Just in case you need a little extra encouragement, here's Mackenzie's story told in her own words.

"My husband and I are chiropractors and own our own business. We had been struggling since opening our practice, so my husband took a full-time job as a chiropractor at another office so that our finances would be more stable. I was six-months pregnant when we bought the practice, and I had to take an unexpected extended maternity leave after the baby was born. I really struggled with going back to work, wanting to stay home with my new daughter, and generally feeling overwhelmed with trying to get our practice going on my own with limited time and resources.

"After much soul-searching, I came to realize that I did want to continue working and helping people through the natural healing arts. But I just felt as though I couldn't get things moving and off the ground. I was trying so hard and getting nowhere.

"Then I was introduced to The Soul-Math Formula. It was such a godsend. I knew I had been getting in my own way, but I didn't understand what exactly I was doing to hinder my own progress and success.

"With the help of a mentor familiar with the formula, I was able to unearth some deeply held personal beliefs of unworthiness and inability to handle the gift of having my own practice. I realized that while I believed that the Universe was abundant, flowing, and available for me, I felt that I had let God down; that I had messed up in the past, disappointed God (and myself), and simply didn't earn or deserve the blessings in my life. It was a real revelation to me that I held this to be true. It was painful to uncover these facts, but so very powerful and productive."

Dr. Mackenzie's Diagnostic Worksheet

Sample Worksheet

The Soul-Math™ Formula

Dr. Mackenzie's Diagnostic Worksheet

1. Existing circumstance needing correction: *My chiropractic business is failing*   **Date:**

3. Record your typical thoughts as they relate to #1.	4. Record your typical emotions and feelings as they relate to #1.	5. What do you believe as related to #1? Dig Deep!	6. Record current patterns of action and behavior.	2. How are things now? What is the result you are experiencing?
Thought x	**Feeling** x	**Belief** x	**Action** =	**Present Situation**
I need more patients. Not enough resources. I don't know how to market the practice. It's hard to charge for my services. Not enough time or energy. I am not enough. I have to do it alone. I didn't sign up for this. I want to be successful. I want to help people. I owe my family so much! I want to make them proud. My husband has to work another job for now. Location is undesirable. I'm sacrificing time with my baby to work. I am failing	I am overwhelmed. I am unworthy. Resentful my husband can't help me more. Guilty, embarrassed for not being successful yet. Alone, lonely, dumb. Unqualified, inadequate. I overcomplicate things. I've lost the joy for this. I miss my husband. I don't have any fun. (Positives) I am blessed to set my own schedule. I have opportunity to create the practice of my dreams! I love the time I have to spend with my baby.	I have to do it all myself. I can't ask for help. I don't deserve to have my Own practice. I'm not good enough. I'm not doing enough. I don't know enough. There's not enough time. People won't want to pay for my services. People won't go out of their way to come here. I don't believe in myself. I'm messing things up. I'm being judged. I'm disappointed in myself and God is, too.	I am spinning my wheels. Ineffective marketing. State of indecision. Unfocused. I pick fights with my husband. I am frustrated with my baby and myself. I avoid scheduling new patients. I have trouble asking for payment. The patients that I do have are great and are happy with their care.	My chiropractic business is failing. I am seeing 3 patients per week. My husband has to work at another office because our business is so slow. I work limited hours because I have a new baby.

"Phylis teaches that when you work through a transforming process like The Soul-Math Formula, you then proceed to vision and plant your 'prayer-seed' in the soil of Universal Intelligence, like you would plant an acorn in the ground expecting an oak tree. You then have to let the seed grow without digging it up every day to see if it's working! With faith and patience, you'll find that a great tree will be produced if given the time to develop and grow. So that's what I did. I worked through the diagnostic worksheet and uncovered my hidden BS (belief system) and blocks that were stopping me from claiming the blessings in my life. I also worked through a correction worksheet for my problem. I wrote down the new thoughts, feelings, beliefs, actions, and results that I wanted and needed to accomplish my goal of having a successful, thriving, and service-driven practice. I planted the seed and was quickly back to my busy life of being a new mom and business owner."

Dr. MacKenzie's Correction Worksheet

Sample Worksheet

The Soul-Math™ Formula
Dr. Mackenzie's Correction Worksheet

1. Existing circumstance needing correction: *My chiropractic business is failing*   **Date:** _____

3. Record your highest thoughts that would be in support of #2.	4. Record your highest emotions that would be in support of #2.	5. Record your highest beliefs that would be in support of #2.	6. What would patterns of action be like in support of #2?	2. State desired result.
Thought x	**Feeling x**	**Belief x**	**Action =**	**Present Situation**
I have a daily/weekly plan. Systems are in place. Marketing plan unfolding. Business management easier. People value my services. There's plenty of time. I am awesome and successful! I am NOT alone. I am a huge success. I am helping people every day. It's easy to get to this office. My family is proud and knows I am working hard to repay them. My life is balanced and happy. Our business is thriving and growing every day. My husband is ready to quit his other job because our practice is ready to support us!	Calm, in control. Empowered. Worthy. Peaceful. I feel confident. I am deeply satisfied with my life, my marriage, and my business. I love my patients. I love my business. I have a plan. I follow it, and it feels so good! I feel proud of myself. I am filled with joy and have fun at the office. I trust myself. I am fully supported. I feel blessed to have such an incredible family. I feel overjoyed that my dreams are becoming a reality.	I don't have to do this all by myself. I am fully supported. I am worthy of all good. I am proud of the job I'm doing. I take ownership of our business. People gladly travel to our office and value the service. I am using all of my gifts and skills in the perfect way. Life is wonderful! I am deeply grateful for my family's help. My family is proud of me! I believe in me and know that God is always with me every step of the way!	Systems are in place that make working easy. I am eagerly learning new marketing skills. I am easily managing my growing business. I wake up every morning grateful and focused. My husband and I are enjoying each other. I enjoy quality time with my daughter. I have new systems for scheduling and working with new patients. I let God into my life and feel loved and cared for. I take action to create a life that is happy, balanced and fulfilling.	My chiropractic business is a huge success! Our business is thriving. I am booked with patients every day. I am helping so many people and feel joyful and satisfied in so many ways. My husband is back at our office full-time. We are financially sound and paying back our family. We've found a perfect balance of work and family time.

"What happened next came as a huge surprise. Within TWO weeks, I had six new patients! I was booked with several patient visits each day. We had a new massage therapist join our practice and contribute income to nearly half of our overhead! Suddenly, my phone was ringing each day with new patients interested in coming in to see me. I made more money in those two weeks than I had made in almost the first year of practice. I truly believed that the revelations made possible by The Soul-Math Formula would work. I just never dreamed my seed would grow into a beautiful tree so quickly! It has been such an incredible blessing. My husband and I are making plans for him to finally leave his other job and come back to our office full-time, and life has never felt so good!

"I am so filled with gratitude for the changes that have already manifested in our lives. Before this exercise, I thought that God and the Universe were accessible and always working toward our highest good, but now I know it. I feel it in my soul."

CHAPTER 13

FINAL NOTES ON SOUL-MATH™

Bad times have a scientific value.
We learn geology the morning after the earthquake.
—Ralph Waldo Emerson

The Thought Factor

HERE'S SOMETHING TO remember about yourself as you dig into your psyche. You rarely produce a truly new thought with respect to making choices and decisions. Why? Because most of the time you simply reorganize stored information, or habits of thought. You keep reshuffling the same deck of cards! To create something truly different, you need a *new* deck of cards. In other words, you need to break out of addictive patterns of thinking and forge a new path of awareness and intention.

The question is, how miserable and afraid do you have to become before you're willing to monitor and change your thoughts? The answer is different for each person. Just use the creative process in a positive way, understanding you *must* be willing to change thoughts that no longer serve you by producing new ones that support better results.

What thoughts should you shoot for in order to launch a corrective and creative road toward happiness and fulfillment? You should always shoot for the highest possible *positive* thoughts. When you think you've done this, go higher. And then go even higher. But you might say, "Well, okay,

I'll change this thought, and this thought, but not *that* thought. I could never change my mind about *that*." The truth is you can change anything you *want* to change.

To get to where you want to be from where you are now, you must begin by consciously changing your thoughts to match your grandest vision. *The thoughts that created a problem in your life can't possibly be the thoughts that will create a solution to that problem.*

So are all thoughts creative in and of themselves? No. Only those thoughts that are charged by the fire of feelings.

The Feeling Factor

Your heart often knows things before your mind does.
—Polly Adler

The relationship of the *feeling factor* to the *thought factor* in The Soul-Math Formula is like an electrical spark to a spark plug. Feelings are the energies that move you in response to your thoughts and experiences. Without the emotions, thoughts and experiences would remain neutral. Feelings are the yeast that makes things happen. Just as thought is mental energy, feeling is emotional energy. Thought may be the beginning of creation, but feelings are the creative urge or impulse. The two go together.

To create anything, or re-create anything, you must learn to manage both your thoughts and your feelings *consciously*. As you learn to lift them to the highest possible level, you will begin to understand the role you play in creating a healthier body, healthier relationships, and a happier experience of life.

The Emotionometer on the following page illustrates the flow of the life force within you when you indulge in the lower emotions, and the flow of the life force when you focus on the higher frequency emotions. Notice that the word *gratitude* is just above the midline. These expressions are key to opening the door to higher energy emotions that support the life urge and lead to happiness and well-being. The next emotion above gratitude and giving is hope, which opens the mind and the heart to new possibilities. There are many more high-level emotions, but these are the basic ones common to most of us. When you get to the top, you reach the highest emotions of unconditional love, peace, and unwavering faith.

Notice that when you experience anger, fear, or situations that throw you into some kind of anxiety, you slide down the Emotionometer time and time again. These emotions are simply energy, and some can be momentarily helpful. For instance, human anger can motivate a person to stand up for him- or herself or what is right, but the anger must be released as soon as its usefulness has run its course. This avoids letting that anger evolve into toxic interference in the body, mind, and spirit. The same is true about fear. A bit of fear can be useful if we find ourselves heading for the edge of a cliff or some other unexpected danger. The key point is to pay attention to these emotions and let them do their job but then move out of them. Do not allow yourself to get stuck in anger or fear. Move into gratitude as quickly as possible and on up the scale.

Emotionometer™

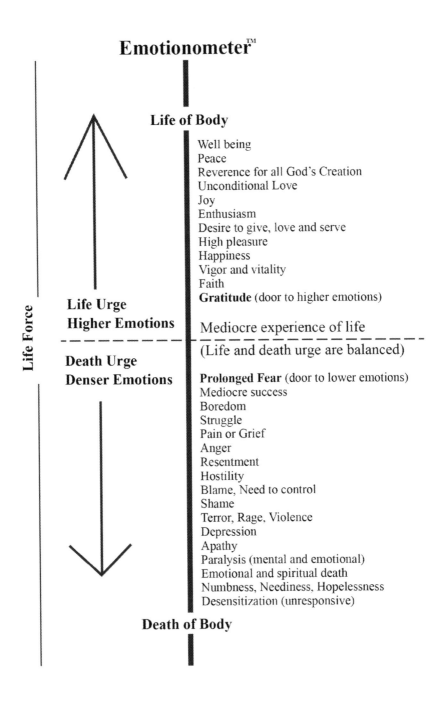

Life of Body

Well being
Peace
Reverence for all God's Creation
Unconditional Love
Joy
Enthusiasm
Desire to give, love and serve
High pleasure
Happiness
Vigor and vitality
Faith
Gratitude (door to higher emotions)

Mediocre experience of life

(Life and death urge are balanced)

Prolonged Fear (door to lower emotions)
Mediocre success
Boredom
Struggle
Pain or Grief
Anger
Resentment
Hostility
Blame, Need to control
Shame
Terror, Rage, Violence
Depression
Apathy
Paralysis (mental and emotional)
Emotional and spiritual death
Numbness, Neediness, Hopelessness
Desensitization (unresponsive)

Death of Body

Life Force

Life Urge
Higher Emotions

Death Urge
Denser Emotions

The Belief Factor

A belief is not merely an idea the mind possesses;
it is an idea that possesses the mind.
—Robert Bolton

Don't short-sell the *belief factor*! Where do beliefs come from? Much of your belief system has been designed by people and things outside of you. Beliefs can literally be programmed into you by family, society, organizations, religious doctrine, or many other sources. Beliefs can be generated by patterns or trends, which means that when something happens enough times in your life, you begin to believe that it will always be true for you.

When you live your life subject to the world around you, you are giving up your power of will to the belief that there are winners and losers, and that you have little or no control over which one you will be. This may have been your perception in the early years of your human experience, but as you grow and evolve, you discover more and more ways to take charge of your own thoughts, feelings, and beliefs.

Belief is a powerful double-edged sword. It has the potential to open your eyes to the real truth or to blind you to the real truth. Through high-level beliefs you can climb the highest mountain; through foolish beliefs you can imprison yourself in ignorance and robotic obedience.

Remember, the effects of the *belief factor* upon the creative process are perhaps the most insidious. Once your thoughts and feelings become a definite belief, that belief takes control and influences your thought and feeling factors to an enormous degree. It thereby affects the action factor as well. Your belief system (BS) literally controls your behavior, self-esteem, and level of happiness.

As you delve into the depths of your consciousness, you want to identify those false beliefs that need correcting. What is a false belief? A false belief is any idea that has become a personal truth for you that is not in alignment with Universal Truth. Here's an example of a false belief. Let's say that John thinks 2 + 2 = 5. In fact, John not only *thinks* it, he really *believes* it. He believes it because his entire family believes it and even the community in which he lives believes it. Now if the community believes it, that community probably thinks the whole world believes it, and more than likely assumes that this belief is a Universal Truth. Even though this belief is an obvious false belief to those outside his community who know the *real* truth, for John and his community this belief is their truth.

The belief that 2 + 2 = 5 is limiting because it forces John to operate within self-imposed boundaries. This causes him to be unaware of anything beyond his faulty belief system. John will never be able to apply the absolute law of mathematics until he corrects the false belief that 2 + 2 = 5. Belief in this equation may be *his* truth, but it is not *the* truth, or absolute truth. His belief is based on a general misperception founded upon ignorance instead of understanding.

The Action Factor

Be not simply good; be good for something.
—Henry David Thoreau

The major purpose of The Soul-Math Formula is to help you explore ways to manage your power of thought, feeling, and belief in a way that compels you to act in a high-intentioned, directed, and motivated way. Action moves you into creation, into production, into self-expression.

Action is a natural step when all the factors are congruent. It places your point of attention upon being, doing, experiencing, radiating, revealing, and manifesting the result you want. Without action, nothing happens in the physical world.

The *action factor* also tells you a lot about your thoughts, feelings, and beliefs. For instance, let's say you had a thought about going back to school to obtain the education necessary to pursue a new career and you got excited just thinking about it. But it's been ten years now, and you've done nothing to move yourself in that direction. Evaluating your actions will help you discover a belief or beliefs that are responsible for holding you back. Perhaps it's a belief that you're too old, not intelligent enough, or some other perceived inadequacy. As you practice making sure your thoughts, feelings, and beliefs are in positive alignment, your actions will be easier to initiate and the results more positive.

The Result

If you would hit the mark, you must aim a little above it;
every arrow that flies feels the attraction of earth.
—Henry Wadsworth Longfellow

My main objective behind sharing both the Forgiveness Process and The Soul-Math Formula in this book is to help you figure out what you must forgive even when you think you have nothing to forgive. But if you continue to struggle with putting actions into play that could change your life, you have forgiving to do as well as changes to make in your thoughts, feelings, and beliefs. Unless you dig out that which is deeply hidden in the subconscious mind, you will more than likely keep throwing up blocks to the freedom that could be yours leading you to happiness, fulfillment, greater peace, and success.

CHAPTER 14

PREVENTING SETBACKS

One doesn't discover new lands
without consenting to lose sight of the shore for a very long time.
—Andre Gide

ONCE YOU TRULY forgive someone and start seeing positive changes in your life, you don't want to have a relapse. And that can happen when you play the blame game. Blaming will lead you down the path of unforgiveness faster than almost anything. And unfortunately, many of us indulge in blame a lot more than we think we do.

We blame the weather. We blame rude drivers. We blame the dog we tripped over, even though he was just lying there. We blame the checkout person at the store for not moving fast enough. We blame our spouse for throwing his black socks in the washer with our new white cashmere sweater. And we blame politicians and world leaders for the state of the world we live in. Although we usually let go of this type of blame pretty quickly, we may still indulge in it and stew about what isn't meeting our expectations. In short, we shut down the opportunity to feel good and maintain a mental and emotional state of well-being.

Now, don't mistake what I'm saying for suggesting we shouldn't have viewpoints that differ from other people. That's what makes the world go round. But when we hang onto blame, or an accusatory state of mind and heart, there's not an ounce of well-being that can squeeze through the low, dense, thick vibration of blame, whether or not it seems justifiable.

A Word of Caution about Moving Forward

When I bring up the subject of moving forward, I'm talking about creating a happy, productive, honest, and fulfilling future. I'm talking about living every present moment in a way that doesn't simply re-create more things to forgive. Unfortunately, most people tend to live their lives in a comfort zone, or a habit pattern, that they've become used to. Even if they don't like the life they're living, there is often a tendency to keep living that life because that's what they're familiar with, that's what they're used to, and they have no clue as to how to move forward in any other way.

A good example are those with low self-esteem who are in the habit of feeling "less than." They may have successfully cleaned up their trail of unforgiveness, but because of their habits, they will almost always create something else to forgive just to prove to themselves how unworthy they are! I've seen this happen over and over again. People can be so addicted to worry, self-pity, being confused about what they really want, or believing they're unworthy that they take a step backward. Then all they get is more of what they thought they'd gotten rid of! And once again they find themselves stuck in the muck of more people, situations, and circumstances, crying out for forgiveness.

Such self-debilitating habits must be stopped! They must be recognized and reversed. This can only be done by making consciousness U-turns. This means shifting your thoughts in a more positive direction, adjusting the emotions to a higher level, cleaning out old beliefs that no longer fit, and taking constructive actions in order to produce healthy, happy, and fulfilling results. Does this mean that everything we experience will be free of challenge? Of course not. Life is full of unexpected, undesirable, and sometimes devastating challenges. But if your thought, feeling, belief, and action patterns are positive, well-intended, and free of obstructions like unforgiveness, low self-worth, worry, or unnecessary fear, life will be generally happy and filled with peace, love, joy, and success.

Redesigning Your Past so You Can Move Forward!

By "redesigning your past" I don't mean that you can change what happened in the past. I'm talking about being able to see the things that happened and the people involved in your past in a new way so you can design your future exactly the way *you* want it rather than allowing the past to control your present. I'm talking about seeing how the past and all the people involved in it, including yourself, have served you in a way that caused you to become conscious about how to move forward with ease rather than struggle.

It's really all about focus. Once true forgiveness or emotional detachment from a memory has taken place, changes in the body and in one's outer experience of life are made possible. This is when it becomes obvious that you have a choice about which memories to focus upon and which ones to let fade into the distance. It then becomes comfortable and even easy to enjoy or learn from the past rather than bemoan and complain about it or forcefully try to forget it.

As you gain a new perspective on things in the past, you will stop wasting your precious present moments reliving the past, talking about it, trying to justify it, or otherwise neutralizing the dynamic possibilities that lie before you.

It also becomes possible to move forward in a new way in order to manifest the self-acceptance, happiness, fulfillment, abundance, love, and peace that's desired. Along with this productive and generally happy life will come the desire to share it with others. As this happens, you will find the greatest freedom you have ever known.

As a result of my personal discovery of the miraculous freedom of true forgiveness and my own power to choose, I was inspired to write the following poem. I hope it speaks to you!

The Greatest Freedom

The greatest freedom is the freedom to choose,
Either this way or that ... to win or to lose.
One chooses laughter, another a frown,
One gets up, while one stays down.
I can choose love or I can choose fear,
You can choose peanuts, I can choose beer.
We can agree or not, however that be,
Because it's our choice that makes us free.

I have to admit I sometimes feel chains
That bind me to anger, or fear, or claims
That "I'm right, you're wrong, *why* can't you see?!
It's all so simple. Just agree with me!"
But then I wake up to the truth of God's grace,
And I know to be free means to honor each place,
Each race, each face, and all things,
And bless every choice ... whatever that brings.

Thank you, God, for the freedom to choose.
To think thoughts of love, or sing the blues.
It's all up to me each moment, each day,
To feel your joy or be willing to pay.
It's always my choice about what to think,
Whether to choose blue or relish hot pink.
It really won't matter, this I know,
Which choice I make or which way I go.

It's all about how I choose to see life,
Through eyes of wonder or feelings of strife.
It's my choice, my decision, as to which way I go,
And the journey will cause me to stumble or grow.
Freedom to me is to honor your voice
Above all others ... that's my choice!
Thank you again for the wisdom to see
What freedom is is up to me.

PART 3

TURNING THINGS AROUND

Men suffer all their life long, under the foolish
superstition that they can be cheated.
But it is impossible for a man to be cheated by anyone but himself.
—Ralph W. Emerson

If you've reached a point where you're now traveling a path of authentic forgiveness, armed with the diagnostic and corrective tools of The Soul-Math Formula, congratulations! You're on your way! Now it's time to take decisive action and create a happier, even more fulfilling life.

At this point, I'd like to remind you, when I use the word *consciousness* I'm referring to your thoughts, feelings, and beliefs—the key components of The Soul-Math Formula. Your consciousness controls and regulates the actions you take, determining the results you experience. And since I know you want great results, I've included in Part Three some additional suggestions, or *consciousness U-turns*, to help you move forward with freedom and ease.

CHAPTER 15

CLEARING THE WAY

*I have always thought the actions of men
the best interpreters of their thoughts.*
—John Locke

Pivot on Adversity

LIFE HAPPENS, SOMETIMES bringing setbacks, other times tragedy. You can bemoan your misfortune—trying to figure out how you attracted such a terrible thing—or you can step back and look at what's happening as an observer rather than as a victim. You can stand frozen in the midst of your disappointment or failure, churning inside over the loss, the mistake you made, or the way you've been treated. Or you can bolster your strength and get your creative juices flowing again by remembering that *you* are in charge of your own thoughts, feelings, beliefs, and actions. You can then find a way to look upon what happened and stop "horriblizing," "awfulizing" and "catastrophizing" about it. In short, you can pivot on adversity and get moving in a positive direction.

The first step is opening your mind and heart to accepting what is. In other words, stop resisting and simply look upon what's happening with a calm sense of detached interest. When facing a difficult situation, a lot of internal struggle comes from a desire to control what's happening and insisting that it be different from what it actually is. But once you relax and accept what is, you can get out of the way and give the problem freedom to move out of your life.

Now when I say accept what is, I'm not suggesting giving up. Quite the contrary. I'm talking about *not attaching* yourself to the adversity. You see, when you fight it, resist it, or push against it, you give it even more energy. Surrender the fight, and you open the door to the possibility of peace. No problem you have ever faced, or will ever face, is bigger than your ability to see it from a higher viewpoint.

In Arabic, the word for "problem" is translated as "another view," suggesting that every difficulty is an invitation to see things from a higher perspective. Again, there is absolutely no problem you could ever face bigger than your ability to see it from a higher viewpoint.

Once you've accepted what is, the next step in pivoting on adversity is to be grateful for those people or situations that challenge you. As the Forgiveness Process suggests, they just could be nudging you to be or do something better.

There's a parable about a farmer who owned an old mule. One day the mule fell into a dried-up well. The farmer could hear the poor animal braying. He could hardly stand listening to the mournful cries of his old friend and frantically tried to figure out what to do. But after a time, the mule became very quiet and still. The farmer assumed he was either dead or injured, and since it seemed impossible to get the mule out of the well, he rounded up his neighbors to help him haul dirt to dump into the well, bury the old mule, and put him out of his misery.

At the bottom of the well, the old mule—who had merely calmed down after its initial fright—stood waiting. It felt some dirt hit its back and shook it off. Then more dirt hit its back. Once again it shook the dirt to the ground. Each time a shovel full of dirt landed on its back, the mule shook it off. Pretty soon, it noticed a big pile of dirt at its feet and instinctively stepped up on it.

The dirt kept coming down the well, and the old mule kept shaking it off and stepping up. Shake it off and step up. Shake it off and step up. Shake it off and step up. Pretty soon, enough dirt had been tossed down the well that the old mule, exhausted but triumphant, was able to climb out of the well—much to the surprise of the farmer and his neighbors.

The point of the story? What seemed would bury the mule actually blessed him because of the way he responded to his adversity. It's the same with us. When we face life's challenges and respond to them positively, refusing to give in to panic, resentment, or self-pity, the innate, built-in power of creativity helps us shake it off and step up.

I know sometimes it's difficult to see the blessing when we find ourselves at the bottom of a deep well. But if nothing else, the situation will teach us to stop repeating the same mistake. In fact, after having had such a challenging experience, we can find the freedom to stand back and laugh at ourselves and the thought of ever again letting such a thing happen.

It's amazing how some of us automatically assume difficulty, adversity, obstacles, and other roadblocks are closing the doors of opportunity. That simply isn't true.

Eckard Tolle, author of *The Power of Now*, writes,

> Whenever any kind of disaster strikes, or something goes seriously "wrong,"—illness; disability; loss of home or fortune or a socially defined identity; break-up of a close relationship; death or suffering of a loved one, or your own impending death—know there is another side to it, that you are just one step away from something incredible: a complete alchemical transmutation of the base metal of pain and suffering into gold. That one step is called surrender.

He's saying that fear and pain can be changed into an inner peace and serenity that comes from a very deep place inside yourself. So remember, when there seems to be no way out—there's always a way through. As you face any challenge, accept what is and short-circuit the temptation to get lost in the pain of what's happening. Then, as you face the challenge, you can maintain a sense of inner calm and composure at the same time. You can shift your perspective so you can see the problem from a different angle and perhaps notice the blessing it's delivering.

Happiness is an acquired skill. If you think you deserve to suffer, it won't matter how wonderful things are, you'll always find something to complain about. Just remember, there's always something to celebrate even in the most difficult times. It's been said that happiness is not so much an outer reality as it is an inner decision. A lot of people are addicted to suffering, and in that state of consciousness, they rob themselves of joy. Don't let yourself be one of them. Pivot on adversity.

Learn to Receive!

I remember sitting at a table in a restaurant with seven or eight people sharing a platter of some wonderful seafood appetizers. At some point, there was just one appetizer left on the platter. So we passed it around, and no one took it. Then a couple of people reached for it at the same time and quickly jerked their hands back when they realized the other person was about to take it. They started saying to each other, "Here, you take it!" "No, you have it!" "That's all right, it's yours!" "No, no, I want you to have it!"

They pushed this appetizer back and forth until they actually started showing some irritation with each other. They both wanted it, but neither one was willing to simply accept it. Finally, the appetizer just sat there, never to be enjoyed by anyone.

What was interesting is that both people showed a genuine effort to be generous, but neither of them could bring themselves to graciously accept from the other person. It's important to always remember that by accepting something, we give the other person an opportunity to practice the art of giving. After all, how could anyone give if there were no one to receive? As the old saying goes, "It's a tough job, but somebody's got to do it!"

It's amazing to me how many people come to counsel with me about a problem they've let immobilize them. They may still be willing to give of themselves to others, often out of obligation, but they shut down their willingness to receive. They can be so stuck in worry, anger, self-pity, confusion, or some other hypnotic emotion that it doesn't even occur to them that a solution, and all the courage and strength they need to move through and beyond the perceived problem, is waiting to be noticed and claimed.

For life to be balanced, there must be a *balance* of giving and receiving. How gracious are you about receiving? Think about how it feels when you offer someone something and the other person isn't willing to receive it. Harve Eker, in his book *Secrets of the Millionaire Mind*, writes, "If you are not willing to receive, then you are 'ripping off' those who want to give to you. You are actually denying them the joy and pleasure that comes from giving."

Always remember, everything is energy. So when you want to give but hold back, the energy of your desire to give can get stuck in your subconscious as guilt or failure or some other suppressed feeling. Likewise, if someone tries to give something thoughtful and kind to you and you push them away, you once again stop the flow of energy and add to unexpressed, stuck emotional goo.

What do we often say when someone gives us a gift? "Oh, you shouldn't have!" Or "It's too much!" Or "This wasn't necessary." Or "You spent too much money on me!" Isn't this really dumping our own feelings of discomfort about receiving on the giver? Isn't this trying to make the giver feel responsible for the problem that *we* have accepting the gift? What if we simply responded with "I'm so surprised and happy about this! Thank you!"

Gratefully accepting tangible gifts or thoughtful kindness from other people isn't the only receiving we must be willing to do. What about the gifts of nature? How often do you open yourself to receive the wonder of a bird, a flower, or a magnificent sunset? What a beautiful way to replenish so you have more to give. As you learn to receive love from your surroundings and the gestures of kindness from other people, the more energized you become.

Remember: you are both a transmitter, or giver, and a receiver. You receive every time you hear someone speak. You receive the feeling of someone's experience, not just from what they say but also by tuning in to what they feel. You receive every time someone touches you. You receive every time you taste the food you're eating. You receive every time you feast your eyes upon nature. You must allow yourself to accept the gifts of life in this way. You must allow yourself to be the receiver you already are.

Some of us feel bad receiving too much because our minds turn to all the people on planet Earth who have so much less than we do. But I encourage you to be mindful about how you regard people in need. Instead of seeing them as poor and needy, see them as wearing their angel wings and giving you an opportunity to give. Hopefully, they will receive *your* kindness and will pass it on by giving to someone else. But however that may be, what they do at that point is their business.

Giving and receiving are both blessings. The law of circulation balances the two. This is one of the most important spiritual principles to understand because this law governs the flow of abundance through your life. Whatever you give out at all levels of your being, whether it be thoughts, intentions, feelings, words, gestures, money, acts of kindness, or material things, will come back to you. But you must be ready and willing to receive. The energy of giving and receiving must flow like a river, so don't dam it up or block its flow by clinging to things you don't need, or hoarding the good that has flowed into your life.

Be the unconditional giver that you're meant to be, and be a worthy, nonresistant, open receiver.

Practice the art of letting the good in!

Clean Up Unfinished Business

Have you ever asked yourself, "Why do I leave so many things hanging until I'm overwhelmed by it all?" Or maybe it's "Why are there so many things in my closet I don't wear?"

You'd be surprised how much of your energy is zapped by unfinished business. And if you're like many people, you leave things undone that are really easy to do. The thing is, every situation, project, or conversation left hanging subconsciously reduces the reserves of your physical, mental, and emotional energy. Of course, you may not realize this until after you've cleaned up some of those loose ends. Then you'll notice how light and free you feel.

You may say, "Well, that's fine, but I have some unfinished business that's beyond my control. I can't do anything about that!" If that's truly the case, and it's totally outside your realm of influence, you can still bring it to a close by releasing it mentally and emotionally. Just make up your mind to let go of it. There's nothing more powerful than a made-up mind. And releasing the situation will let you move forward in your life with lightness and freedom. So stop holding onto something you can't do anything about. That only promotes sustained anger or some other dangerous emotional cliff from which you could fall and hurt yourself. And here's something else to consider. Unfinished business may lead you down the road to self-blame, guilt, or worse. Then you'll not only have those loose ends to clean up but also a lot of self-forgiving to do as well!

So what in your life remains unfinished? What have you intended to get done but haven't? Take an honest look at those things that call for completion. Consider your physical world. What have you been putting off with respect to your physical body? How about your home? Are there legal or financial concerns needing closer attention and completion? What about your future plans? How are your relationships? Are there truths left uncommunicated or lies that need cleaning up? Are there broken promises and agreements you need to acknowledge and resolve? Or perhaps there are acknowledgments you need to make or praise to be given. Make a list, and be thorough. Then methodically and willingly set out to clean up the clutter. And make these things *essential* on your to-do list!

Dare to Lighten Up!

Many of us have become stuck in the drama of life and are far too serious. Instead of smiles and chuckles and belly laughs, we walk around with flat expressions and physical dis-ease. Mark Twain said, "The human race has only one really effective weapon, and that's laughter. The moment it arises, all our hardnesses yield, all our irritations and resentment slip away and a sunny spirit takes their place."

Someone else said, "Love makes the world go round, but it's laughter that keeps us from getting dizzy."

There's nothing in this world that feels better than laughter. When we can't see even a little humor in a situation, it means we're stuck and can't see what's happening from a higher perspective.

I'm sure you've told a funny story about yourself, maybe adding, "It's funny now, but it sure wasn't when it happened!" You laughing about it is an indicator that you've released the situation, freed yourself, and moved on.

You might say, "But sometimes it isn't appropriate or right or possible to laugh at a situation!" Maybe not, but the sooner you lighten up and laugh, the sooner you'll experience relief and release. Laughter is freeing. It stirs up your body's joy chemicals and relieves tension. At the same time, it pushes negative emotional reactions out of the mind and heart, transforming them into acceptance and even appreciation.

Now if you want to be maudlin, sad, fearful, or depressed, that's up to you. But remember: "Those who enjoy being on the train, and those who *do not* enjoy being on the train, get to the same destination at the same time."

In an episode of *Star-Trek*, Captain Kirk and Mr. Spock were trapped behind an invisible barrier that could not be penetrated. They looked through the barrier helplessly watching their friend, Dr. McCoy, being beaten to a pulp before their eyes. They could do nothing to save him.

Captain Kirk became more and more angry and frustrated and shouted, "We've got to do something! We can't just let him die while we stand here and watch!"

Now Mr. Spock—always the voice of reason—very clearly and firmly said, "Perhaps there IS something we can do, Captain. But I believe it may not be exactly in the way that you are thinking."

"What is it?" replied Captain Kirk.

"I wonder, Captain, if this wall that is stopping us is one of your own creation?"

"What are you talking about, Spock? Out with it!"

"Well, Captain, this force field stopping us may be a result of the wild emotional energy that you are generating. It appears the angrier you get, the thicker the wall becomes. Perhaps if you relaxed and let go of your sympathizing with the doctor's pain, the wall might weaken, and we could then go to the Doctor's aid."

"Alright, Spock, it's worth a try. What shall I do?"

"Simply put your emotions aside for a few moments. Lighten up, Captain. Understand we cannot help the doctor by anxiously worrying about him. Enter a clear state of mind in which emotions have no hold over you. This, I believe, is our only avenue of escape."

The captain closed his eyes and did what Spock suggested. As he did, the force field began to weaken and diminish.

"It's working, Captain, please continue," said Spock.

Within a few minutes, the wall disappeared, and the crew was free to release their friend, Dr. McCoy.

Like Captain Kirk, we, too, can build walls between our current, uncomfortable circumstances and what we desire if we allow our emotions to get the best of us. We can let them lift us up to enjoy great living or keep us trapped behind a wall of pain and frustration.

It's important to realize that overfocusing on counterproductive emotions like fear, anger, resentment, guilt, unworthiness, or loneliness do not produce harmony or inner peace. Nor do they help create joy and satisfaction in your life. And they most certainly do not assist you in making the kind of contribution that a lighthearted, clear-headed, happy person can offer to him- or herself as well as to the world.

CHAPTER 16

FOCUS, FOCUS, FOCUS

Belief consists in accepting the affirmations of the soul,
unbelief, in denying them.
—Ralph Waldo Emerson

Affirmations That Really Work!

AFFIRMATIONS ARE GENERALLY thought of as positive statements to help us convince ourselves that something we want to be true is true. They're used to help us maintain patience and a healthy trust that a vision we have in mind is in the process of actually happening. From my point of view, there is a problem with this perspective. I've noticed over the years that as people use positive affirmations, sometimes they help and sometimes they don't. Why? Because an affirmation and the consciousness of the person leaning on it for support may not be compatible.

Here's a good example. I once knew someone who walked around for years repeating the affirmation, "I am a mighty money magnet making millions!" Never happened. He was just spewing out words his belief system automatically kicked out every time he said them! You see, when we have an idea or vision in mind of what we want, sometimes we have to sneak up on our belief system to convince it to change. In the case of the Mighty Money Magnet, he was jumping way outside his own "consciousness container," which includes his belief system.

Our consciousness container operates like a comfort zone. If we introduce something that reaches way beyond what we believe is possible, our belief system immediately kicks it out as being uncomfortable, unrealistic, and ridiculous. It's as if our belief system is laughing at us! So does that mean affirmations don't work? No. We just have to gradually convince our belief system to accept the changes we want to make. It's like stretching our comfort zone gradually to become more and more accepting of greater and grander desires and intentions. Like I said, we have to gradually sneak up on it. So following is the way to construct your positive affirmations that will actually work:

"Up until now I have believed _____.
But every day it's becoming easier and easier to _____."

It's that simple. For example, "Up until now I've believed the most I deserve to earn as a yearly income is $75,000. But every day it's becoming easier and easier to believe myself worthy of manifesting an income of $95,000 or better!"

How does that feel? If it still feels like a stretch, pick a number you feel more comfortable with—one you can accept as realistic and fits with your current self-value registered in your belief system. Then it won't be kicked out. Later, once you've reached that goal, feel free to stretch it out a bit more. You're sneaking up on your BS!

Here's another example: "Up until now I've believed people always leave me. But every day it's becoming easier and easier to attract people who are compatible, faithful, and dependable."

Get the idea? Simple, right? Affirmations like these are extremely helpful in making consciousness U-turns. Just be sure to be persistent, positive, and patient when using them.

Staying in "the Zone"

Ask any athlete how he or she performs so well and that person usually talks about getting into "the zone." Athletes who are "in the zone" are focused on taking the perfect action necessary to win or excel. They see themselves crossing the finish line or running into the end zone with a touchdown. And they see themselves doing it with ease.

Getting into "the zone"—finding that focus— is just as important for us if we want to improve our game of life. So what does that mean? It means, like an athlete, we need to "get in the flow," or in the present moment, tuning out any distractions that might stop us from achieving our ultimate goal—a happy, productive life.

Of course, the zone is even more than just the present moment. It's the present moment free from the baggage of the past and fear of the future. It's the present moment during which you are fully awake and aware. This is the New Now, the working unit of your life. It's fresh, innocent, uncontaminated by judgment or analysis. The environment of the new now is the unlimited sea of possibility.

So as much as possible, go beyond the enslavement of time and live in the present moment—the only time you really have. Think about it. This New Now moment is all there is. Be still and notice it. The only thing real for you right here, right now, is that which you're focusing your mind upon. Notice as you read these words, in this present moment, all your needs are met. Everything you need you have in this moment. As that sinks in, notice how relaxed, safe, and peaceful you feel as you realize that this present moment is full of ideas, inspiration, and possibility. Feel the peace of this moment. You're not resisting anything or thinking about anything except how free you feel right now. Welcome to "the zone."

When I ask people to do this in a private session or in groups, someone occasionally comes up with the comment, "Well, not every one of my present moments is all that great! In fact, some of them are stressful and horrible. What about *those* precious present moments? Sometimes they feel more like the Twilight Zone!" If that's the case, maybe you need to go back to The Soul-Math Formula to uncover the belief that's producing such a negative outlook. Or perhaps you have more forgiving to do! Remember, whatever challenging moment you find yourself in, you have the power of choice to decide how to make the best use of that moment. You can see the situation in a negative way or choose a new thought, feeling, belief, and action that will carry you through to the next moment with power and strength.

One day I sat at my desk attempting to work, but my mind kept drifting off into the Land of Dread that surrounded an upcoming dental appointment. Every time I became conscious of my thoughts sliding off into fear, I pulled myself back into the zone. I did a pretty good job of it. That is until the time of the actual appointment.

Stretched out in my dentist's chair was a present moment that didn't seem so precious. And there I would remain for almost eight hours! That's 28,800 seconds, or consecutive present moments! I was filled with panic. My stomach tightened, my heart began pounding, and my breathing almost stopped. The procedure began along with the pain. My body tensed as I anticipated each subsequent painful moment. I was out on the fragile limb of future moments. And I was out there all alone.

Then I remembered the comment, "Not every one of my present moments is all that great! Some of them are stressful and horrible!" And I realized that I had the perfect opportunity to experiment with and practice what I'd been teaching. With every ounce of conscious awareness I could muster, I brought myself back into the present moment, into the anxiety and the aching neck, aware of the masked face bending over me and the gloved hands that invaded my mouth. Could this be the soul-zone I had been so highly recommending?

I did some strong self-talk and allowed the big chair to become an all-encompassing, loving, caring angel. I let a sense of peace and harmony fill my body, imagined it filling the doctor, and let it fill the present moment. I allowed my body to relax, let go of the fear, and surrendered to the physical reactions to what was happening. As I relaxed more and more, I was able to begin mentally and emotionally stepping from moment to moment, always staying in the zone. I was able to create a new experience for each New Now moment. I simply took my essence somewhere else. I created mind-pictures of other places—a beach at sunset and a redwood forest. It was a 480-minute trip to exotic places.

When the procedure was finished, I returned to the dental chair. Everyone around me looked exhausted and was amazed at how well I came through the experience. In case you're wondering, the answer is yes, I did get up to use the bathroom a couple of times. But each time I returned, I climbed back into my own personal teleporter and took off to another peaceful, safe place.

My experience that day showed me even more clearly that we always have the power we need to reshape or change the moment. So does that mean it's possible to spend every moment in the zone? Perhaps. But because this world is a dimension of learning and remembering, you'll more than likely find yourself drifting in and out. Sometimes you'll fall back into the law of averages—subject to the toss of the dice. In a time like that you may even begin feeling sorry for yourself. It's okay. It happens to all of us. There are times when we're in the flow and times when we're focused only on the obstructions. But on days that aren't exactly flowing, you might notice that the universe has a way of offering you opportunities to reenter the zone free and clear.

I remember having a down day for no particular reason. It was so bad the thought didn't even occur to me to pray or meditate. I went shopping instead, hoping to shake off my self-pitying mood. At the shopping center, I parked my car, got out, and started walking toward the store entrance. As I approached the door—right in the middle of some self-indulgent thought—a man in a wheelchair rolled past me with a lap full of his purchases and no legs below the knees. As I watched, he rolled across the parking lot and disappeared among the cars.

I stopped in my tracks, letting the zone impact me. But I didn't react to what I saw with sympathy or sadness. The thought that came to me was one of gratitude. My entire attitude of mind shifted to one of freedom, lightness, and joy. That man, wearing his angel wings, showed up for me at just the right time. Thank goodness I was awake enough to see him and get his message: "Count your blessings, Phylis. Stop indulging in self-pity and get busy being your best self!" And I did just that.

The zone is *present-time consciousness*. Being *in* the zone is being *awake* and *alert* and *aware* in the present moment, *noticing* what's in the present moment with you. Always notice the intuitive impulses. Notice the meaningful coincidences that show up to guide you. As you become more acutely awake and aware in the present moment, you will *engage the flow*. As you spend more time in the zone, you will build confidence in the truth that everything you need is in the present moment with you. Fear diminishes and freedom abounds.

Don't become Polarized!

Have you ever thought to yourself, "Life is unfair" or "I just don't see a way out of this?" If so, you're anchoring yourself in an opinion, attitude, or perspective that is rigid and inflexible. In short, you're positioning. Positioning is a form of stubbornness that sets up expectations and assumptions, and places conditions upon whatever it is you're positioning yourself for or against. It can be a position of critical judgment or a defensive, political, or unforgiving position. Whatever form it takes, positioning puts you in slow motion, keeping you anchored in place, unable to make any positive changes. It's incredibly polarizing.

Of course, by polarizing I'm not talking in terms of magnetic or ionic polarity, but in terms of emotional and mental polarity—an extreme position separate from any other possibility. If you have a polarized consciousness, you are focused on your own competitive, controlling position or personal viewpoint.

Many people polarize themselves by taking a position, such as "Life just dealt me a bad hand" or "Everyone is against me." This position separates them from any possibility of finding common ground or a solution leading them back toward happiness and success. Remember, there's always a way out of any seemingly dreadful circumstance.

True, life isn't fair. But it's also true that life isn't unfair. It just is. It's what you do with it mentally and emotionally that determines your experience of it. If you feel sorry for yourself, you position yourself as a victim of circumstances by complaining about what's wrong with factors outside yourself. You might find yourself telling your story to friends or anyone who will listen to elicit their sympathy. Of course, all this does is reinforce self-pity and supports your position. It's when you move out of the position that life is unfair, drop the self-pity, and take action to do the best you can with what you have that things begin to change. You "depolarize" yourself into possibilities and opportunities.

Moving out of positioning also keeps you from feeling sorry for other people. When you stop feeling sorry for others, you no longer experience feelings of helplessness, condescension, superiority, or pity. Instead, you graduate to compassion, a place of heartfelt emotion that conveys empathy, kindness, and understanding to everyone around you. It enables you to recognize and honor the uniqueness and strengths in others that can see them through their difficulties. By all means, if it is within your realm of influence to be of assistance to someone, do it. But as you do, practice substituting the phrase, "I have compassion for that person" in place of "I feel sorry for that person." Compassion and sincere caring moves you out of victim consciousness and into constructive action.

So what are some of the stubborn positions in which you have anchored yourself? Perhaps it's "My way is the only way," "All men are alike," or "All women are gossips." Maybe it's something like "The world is a scary place" or "I'll never amount to anything" or "That's just the way I am." The specifics of your positioning aren't the most important thing here. The most important thing is to realize that you may be holding onto many ideas that glue you in place so you don't get anywhere beyond your position. Giving up or softening your judgments and positions will not make you disappear into a nonentity or cause you to crumble into a lifeless blob. Giving up your critical judgments and positions will get you moving.

If you want to see just how much you're judging and polarizing yourself, go back to The Soul-Math Formula. It won't take long to see exactly how you may be limiting your experience of life.

Gratitude Therapy

Gratitude is a key that can open many locked doors that may be interfering with your forward movement. It's one of the magic wands that create a miracle mind-set. It's the opening that lets love in. It can change the mental lens through which you view the world and move you up the ladder of emotion into hope, faith, joy, unconditional love, and finally, profound peace. And it's absolutely essential to your happiness.

Gratitude is one of the most effective therapies you can apply to your mind and heart. To whom or to what are you to be grateful? To the God of your understanding. To Universal Intelligence. To life itself.

As you apply the magic wand of gratitude, it will soothe your wounds, heal your hurts, lift your spirit, and inspire your soul.

Routinely, someone comes into my office with feelings of dissatisfaction about their job. It seems more and more vital for them to find fulfillment and personal meaning in what they do. Some tell me how important it is for them to do something to serve others. But I can see they *already are* doing a job that serves others in some way. I think what they're really saying is, they want to do something meaningful to, and in service to, themselves.

I'm sure you know people who go to work every day and do the kind of job that some might consider meaningless. Maybe they work on an assembly line, doing the same thing over and over. Or perhaps they work as a cook, making hundreds of hamburgers in a day. And yet some of these people seem happy, and some seem surly and resentful.

If you were to ask the happy workers how they do that boring, meaningless job all the time, they probably wouldn't say, "It *is* a meaningless, boring job. I have no idea how I manage. But then it's the best I can do." Nope, not the happy people. If those people are happy inside, they've found meaning in that job. And they may answer your question by saying, "My job isn't meaningless. It earns me a living. I have responsibilities to meet and rent to pay. Besides, there's no stress, and I enjoy the rhythm of what I do."

It also could be that this happy person is seeing beyond the obvious justification of what he's doing, realizing what he does on that assembly line makes the product safe for others to use. And the person making the hamburgers may get a great deal of satisfaction from the smile on people's faces when they keep coming back for more.

The point is, if you haven't already made up your mind to be happy and fulfilled right now where you are, a new job isn't going to make any difference. You'll find it difficult to find meaning anywhere. Of course, that doesn't mean you have to stay in the same job forever. By all means, if you're not satisfied with your work, look for something else. Just remember when choosing that new job, choose from a place of gratitude.

Shifting into an attitude of gratitude will help you see the meaning in whatever you do. What's more, it opens the door to joy and prepares you to receive more and more blessings.

I've heard it said that some people who do an excellent job 98 percent of the time belittle themselves for the other two percent. I wonder how many of us fall into that pattern of self-abuse. It's vital to retrain your mind to focus on what *is* working rather than what is *not* working, to move the spotlight of attention away from your imperfections to your abilities and then expand on that.

If you're stuck in the habit of faultfinding, it's something you've learned, not something you were born with. But you can rewire your mind to find a sense of gratitude about everything. When you first wake up in the morning, your mind is more open to receive new impressions. So one of the best things you can do is take responsibility for your thoughts and feelings first thing each morning.

On the other hand, if you want to decrease your chances for happiness that day and your ability to move forward, listen to the morning news while you brush your teeth or drink your cup of coffee. Don't let anything get by you! Keep tabs on everything—the economy, wars, rapes, murders, bombings, gossip, and disasters. But if you want to experience a day filled with miracles, sit down and hang out in grateful silence for a few minutes every morning. Review the gratitude in your heart. Ready yourself with gratitude for the wonderful day ahead.

Every day is a special and glorious day, and your presence on the planet is a wonderful gift. So today, and throughout this week, practice waving your magic wand of gratitude until you make it a habit. Think about the people who have loved and supported you. Think about the blessings you've received, the beauty you behold every day, the strength you have, the wisdom you have accumulated, and the visions you have manifested.

Give thanks for your health, abundance, talents, creativity, and ability to laugh, walk, talk, see, hear, taste, and smell. If you are challenged in one or more of these things, give thanks for the challenges and the willingness to rise above them and focus on that which is good, that which is true, and that which offers you an opportunity to be the best you you can be. Then watch the miracles happen.

CHAPTER 17

NO-NO'S

Even if you are on the right track, you'll get run over if you just sit there.
—Will Rogers

Don't Put on the Brakes!

LIFE CAN HAVE a wonderful flow to it when that flow isn't interfered with or shut off. By flow I don't mean to imply that every moment in life can or should be perfect. Everyone experiences pitfalls, backslides, mistakes, and challenges, both large and small. But it's possible to learn the art of nonresistance by *accepting what is* and facing that experience with wisdom, compassion, detached interest, and a willingness to see beyond or through a challenge to what it will be like on the other side. A challenging experience can be like walking through a dark tunnel seeing a bright light at the end of it, and it isn't a freight train! A helpful, comforting thought is "This too shall pass."

The important thing is, when you get to the other side of a challenge and the flow starts moving at a comfortable pace, don't stop it. Don't sabotage yourself. Don't put your foot on the hose. Don't put on the brakes! Just let the flow move along without interference!

I see this come up time after time in classes about manifesting one's dreams. For instance, someone might have serious goals about building and expanding their business. But even after following my recommendations and seeing some wonderful results, I hear them say things like "Now I have so much business, I can't handle it all!" That's putting on the brakes! And before they know it, business drops off and they're back where they started. Either that or they find themselves miserable instead of happy!

Here's where I find many people putting on the brakes. When they finally get clear about how they want to carry out their life purpose, they aren't willing to make necessary changes. So ask yourself, "What must I *be* in order for my vision to become a reality?" This is important because you'll never create something you're not willing to embody. Remember what you learned as we discussed The Soul-Math Formula? You'll always manifest according to the content of your consciousness. Your consciousness shapes your reality. Your consciousness is who you demonstrate in the manifest world. The Soul-Math Formula is invaluable in helping you reveal the content of your consciousness and the ways you must change it in order to bring forth your vision.

The definition of "flow," according to The American Heritage Dictionary, is to move or run smoothly with unbroken continuity. It means to proceed steadily and easily. "The flow" refers to a steady stream of good moving through us and into our world of experience. It means ease instead of struggle, grace instead of awkwardness, and an inner rhythm that pours itself through our choices, decisions, and intentions.

Now there are many things that can stop the flow of good in our lives—doubt, fear, low self-worth, worry, resistance, or a belief in scarcity. These thoughts, feelings, and beliefs that chatter on and on in our heads are contrary to that which constitutes personal power, strength, courage, and trust in the Universal Intelligence in which we live and move and have our being.

All ego negativity that gives power to outside forces rather than connecting with the true power of inner forces and the good at the core of our being will act as shut-off valves to the flow of prosperity, abundance, love, peace, happiness, and joy—what we truly desire.

Oh, we might think what we want is a job, a new car, a better house, more money, or something else from that endless list of dreams and desires. But if you'll notice, once you get the thing you've wanted and the newness wears off, you're ready to chase after the next thing. It's a vicious cycle of trying to satisfy an insatiable need for more. I believe what every person *really* wants is to feel loved, loving, lovable, peaceful, joyful, and satisfied. We must do whatever is necessary to cultivate and experience these feelings first as we go about pursuing our dreams and desires. That's when the flow keeps flowing!

It's fine to *want* things. But when we understand that it isn't the *things* that make us happy, we can enjoy the journey of life and bring our joy to everything we do. This makes manifesting our desires easy instead of a struggle. When we're already happy, it's so much easier to feel gratitude for all the wonderful things that bless our lives.

Misery Has Enough Company!

Out of curiosity one day, I googled the phrase "I hate my life!" I was amazed at how many blogs and websites came up, all offering ways for people to share their misery, vent their anger, tell their tales of woe, and wallow in the goo of self-pity, hate, and unforgiveness. There were even bumper stickers for sale, stating "I Hate My Life!" Obviously, these blogs prove the old cliché, "Misery loves company." Well, my feelings are, misery has enough company!

Over the years I've counseled a number of people who, at least temporarily, think they hate their lives. I remember one person who used to come see me for spiritual counseling at least once a month to rehash and recall all her troubles. It never failed. She'd repeat the same set of complaints over and over again, having memorized them to the point where she could recite them the same way every time! It was as if she were using our time together to rehearse her misery. Because of my experience with this person, I was blessed with the vivid realization that endlessly rehearsing your troubles won't get you anywhere. The fact is, you will never learn to love life and feel happy unless you *decide* you want to feel happy, start rehearsing happy stories of gratitude and possibility, and spend time around happy people. At some point, I told this person that I could do nothing for her without her cooperation and willingness to give up her misery. I often wonder how she's treating life these days!

It's sad, but like a computer that defaults to a certain setting, some of us have a "misery default." And if we don't reset our minds and hearts, we'll spiral down that slippery slope into despair and unforgiveness. Resetting our minds and hearts could mean many things, depending upon our willingness to change things once we realize we needn't walk around with a "misery default" setting.

So how do you identify yourself? Try this. With one hand, point to yourself. Now notice where you're pointing. I'll bet you're not pointing at your head or your back or your arm or leg! My bet is you're pointing to the general area of your heart, as if to say, "This is me! Here I am!" It's not uncommon for someone overwhelmed with good or bad news to place a hand on their chest near their heart. We also do it if we feel awestruck, or filled with wonder. And if terribly hurt by something someone has said, we often protect our heart with our hand.

Most of us identify a lot more with the heart than we do with the head. When was the last time you told someone you love him or her with all of your head? Or told your lover you wanted to give your brain to him or her? And when was the last time you gave someone brain-shaped candy on Valentine's Day? The heart is the seat of our emotional nature. Not only that, but in the last twenty years there's been a lot of validating research to say we actually *think* with the heart as well as with the head. You might recall the Bible verse, Proverbs 23:7, "As a man thinketh in his heart, so is he."

When we think with the heart, with thoughts wrapped in love, we find ourselves in tune with higher, freer emotions. That's when we feel happy. And what a gift it is to feel so good! It's impossible to feel good and miserable at the same time. Misery has enough company. Go find other people who feel good, who are happy, and spend your valuable present moments in their company.

Of course when you find yourself in the presence of someone happier or more successful than you, you can respond in one of two ways. You can celebrate that person for showing up as an example and inspiration for you—showing you the possibility that you, too, can manifest happiness and success. Or you can believe you're stuck, locked in misery—with no power to change things for yourself. The second choice only adds to your misery, causing you to resent the happy person for having what you don't have.

If you happen to feel you're holding onto some misery, the two questions you must ask yourself are "Do I really want to give up this stuck state I've been in for so long? Is there perhaps some kind of *payoff* for staying right where I am, willing to sacrifice my own happiness?"

People choose to stay stuck for many reasons, mostly unconscious ones. They may stay stuck because they're afraid of changing even for something better. Many people become addicted to the attention their misery brings them. And they may be unwilling to change their positioning—using their misery to manipulate others. They also may be unwilling to truly forgive. This is, of course, where the Forgiveness Process and The Soul-Math Formula can work wonders!

Try catching yourself every time you start talking about some past incident that caused you pain or hurt. Then stop it. Try catching yourself when you start *matching* someone's misery that they're telling you about. Then stop it. Recognize the pattern. Admit and recognize the "stuckedness" and create within your own mind a new intention. An intention to move on. An intention to heal. An intention to change your life. An intention to be happy and attract other happy people. Work The Soul-Math Formula and dig up the beliefs you didn't realize were controlling you and prolonging your misery. Misery has enough company!

Don't Accept the Gift!

I know this sounds contradictory after telling you earlier about the importance of being willing to receive. But the fact is, sometimes people try to give us unkind, hurtful gifts like criticism or anger. These are the gifts you *don't* want to receive!

There's a legend that perfectly illustrates how to deflect those verbal or emotional attacks without fighting back, arguing, or otherwise polluting your own consciousness. It's about an aged Samurai warrior who, although still quite capable of defeating any adversary, now preferred to spend his days teaching young people the art of peaceful living.

One afternoon, a strong and powerful young warrior, known for his unscrupulous behavior and habit of striking back at anyone who offended him, came upon the old Samurai teaching a group of students.

Aware of the old Samurai's reputation as a mighty warrior, the young warrior, wanting to further his own legend, challenged the old Samurai with the intention of soundly defeating him. To the great surprise of his students, the old Samurai accepted the challenge.

As news of the challenge spread, a crowd began to gather. Smugly, the young warrior began taunting the old Samurai, throwing rocks at him and spitting in his face. The insults and abuse went on for hours with the young warrior doing everything he could to provoke the old man. But the old Samurai remained calm and unresponsive. Finally, feeling exhausted and humiliated by the old Samurai's refusal to pick up his weapon, the young warrior left.

As the crowd dispersed, the old Samurai's students crowded around him, disappointed and a bit angry that he had allowed such insults to be heaped upon him with no thought of retaliation. "How could you take so much abuse and indignity?" they cried. "Why didn't you pull your sword? How could you display your cowardice in front of us all?"

The old Samurai calmly looked at the students and replied, "If someone comes to you with a gift, and you do not accept that gift, to whom does the gift belong?"

The students became silent. Finally, after much consideration, one spoke up. "The gift would belong to he who tried to deliver it."

"Exactly," said the old Samurai. "If someone comes to you with the gift of envy, anger, and insults, do not accept them. If not accepted, they still belong to the one who carried them in the first place."

What a wonderful lesson! If we can just learn to follow this wise man's example, we, too, can deflect unkind attacks and keep ourselves free to experience peace instead of the mental and emotional pollution associated with these unwanted "gifts."

If you're interested in another wonderful piece of advice on the subject, take a look at the book *The Four Agreements* by Don Miguel Ruiz. The Second Agreement simply states, "Don't take anything personally." If you follow this, any unwelcome "gift" will remain with the one who presented it to you.

You might also try my method of deflecting unwanted "gifts." Whenever someone hurls sarcasm or anger in my direction, I like to silently use this quote by Terry Cole-Whittaker: "What you think of me is none of my business." Whether you choose this or another method, you will be keeping yourself from storing up toxic emotions that disturb your peace and can contribute to dis-ease in your body.

Watch Your Words!

What pops into your head when I ask, "What are the most powerful weapons in the world—bombs, nuclear missiles?" It's true, these as well as many other weapons of war are extremely formidable. But I suggest to you that the most powerful weapon available to every person on the planet is the tongue that's anchored in the mouth.

We each have a mouth, a tongue, and a voice box. They can be used in wonderful ways, or they can be used as powerful weapons. When you become acutely aware of what's coming out of your mouth, you'll have a good idea of what's really going on in your consciousness. Don't just notice the words themselves but also the tone, the sting, the sharpness, or the kindness. Notice the quality of sincerity or insincerity.

Words may not be powerful when taken by themselves, as in a dictionary, but words are tremendously powerful when they are strung together and become transmitters of thoughts, feelings, opinions, beliefs, and intentions.

With the words we speak, we can make someone laugh or cry. We can lift them up or tear them down. We can speak the truth or spin a yarn, tell a story or tell a lie. Think about how much we take our speech for granted. It comes so naturally, like breathing. And we do so much of it *unconsciously*, rarely realizing how much power we project with our words.

Now the fact that words have incredible power isn't just a lot of baloney. Studies support what I'm saying about the power of words. One of the pioneers who proved this to be true is Japanese professor Masaru Emoto. In his book, *Hidden Messages in Water*, he reported his now famous experiment where he took two glasses filled with water and on one glass wrote "Hate" and on the other wrote "Love." He then froze both glasses of water.

What Emoto discovered when looking at the frozen water samples under a microscope was astounding. The frozen crystals in the glass marked "Hate" were misshapen, deformed, and ugly. But in the glass marked "Love," there was one beautifully shaped crystal after another.

Emoto repeated this experiment several times, and no matter who wrote the words on the glasses or how the letters were reproduced, the results were always the same.

In other experiments, Emoto also found that water from clear springs and water exposed to loving words exhibited brilliant, complex, and colorful snowflake patterns. In contrast, polluted water, or water exposed to negative thoughts, formed incomplete, asymmetrical patterns with dull colors.

This experiment was done over and over in many universities around the world over a ten-year period of time, all manifesting the same results. What does this tell us? It tells us that words carry a vibrational energy. The water responded to that vibrational energy and somehow stored it.

As you become more conscious of the words coming out of your mouth, you will become more conscious about how your internal thoughts and feelings motivate you to say what you say and project what you project. So if you want to make your life even better, pay attention to the self-talk that goes on inside your head that causes you to project those concepts, beliefs, and attitudes with your words. Reprogram yourself with positive and constructive internal conversation.

You have the power to turn the negative into the positive, the bad to the good, and the impossible to the possible just by catching yourself and replacing one thought or feeling with another. Realize that your brain stores the messages you give it as though what you tell it is true, whether true or not.

So start catching yourself when you say things like "Sometimes I think you don't have a brain in your head!" or "You'll be the death of me yet!" or "I could never do that!" or "I am so stupid!" Then realize what you have just said is not the truth. It's a belief or, at best, a thoughtless statement. Then rethink that statement with a positive opposite, or statement of *truth*. Think about your conversations with friends or acquaintances where you end up talking about *how bad things are*. Realize that words that carry fear will project the vibration of fear out into the environment and reinforce your own experience of *how bad things are*. If you have a habit of saying that certain situations or people *make you sick*, don't be surprised if you end up making substantial use of your medical insurance plan.

Remember, words can't be taken back once they're said, and they have the power to change the life of the person to whom they're spoken. I have heard one story after another from people who were told something based on supposition or anger by someone else, and they bought into those words as if they were literally true. Their acceptance of those words still live in their belief system and influence their present lives, even if they were said ten or twenty years ago.

I know someone who heard the words, "Forget it! You don't stand a chance!" They allowed that statement to stick in their minds and hearts, and years later when presented with a possibility for something they deeply desired, they continued to act as if they didn't stand a chance. They didn't pursue that opportunity and to this day have not experienced the joy of a dream unfolding.

Think about how many opportunities you face each day to choose the thoughts you think, the feelings you feel, and the words that come out of your mouth. And follow the words of Don Miguel Ruiz in *The Four Agreements*: "Be impeccable with your word!"

CHAPTER 18

REDESIGNING YOUR FUTURE

Imagination is more important than knowledge.
—Albert Einstein

The Power of Your Imagination

IT'S IMPORTANT TO remember that everything begins with an idea in the mind—a thought. That idea, when supported by high-intentioned feelings and beliefs, tends to become a real thing, event, or experience. That's why it's so important to know what it is you want—what you *really* want. And by the way, for those of you who may have been taught that to desire something is wrong, forget about it! It's okay as long as there's no intention to hurt yourself or anyone else. And here's a real eye-opener: even the desire not to desire is a desire! So if you don't know what you really want, you better get busy figuring it out. Otherwise, you could end up manifesting something less than you deserve or nothing at all! And if you've hidden your desires away because you thought they were wrong, bring them out in the open. It's time they had a chance to see the light— and the power of your passionate imagination!

Okay, once you know what you really want, then what? You get to use your imagination to help bring it to fruition. You see, thought fueled with the feeling of desire is powerful energy, and you shape that energy with your imagination. So if you visualize what it is you truly want as if it's already so, it's likely to manifest in your life.

Imagination is a powerful and valuable tool, without any physical limitations. It adds color, movement, sound, and whatever it takes to bring an idea to life. It's your very own "virtual reality." But this powerful tool must be carefully managed. If allowed to run wild, it can bring up undesirable past memories, conjure up worrisome future events, or escape into a world of fantasy where trouble lurks around every corner. So it's important to learn to use your imagination consciously to create powerful positive images. This is where true forgiveness removes any interference and all your hard work with The Soul-Math Formula comes into play. Use the new insights you've gained through the diagnostic and correction worksheets to create a brand-new vision for your life. And watch the doors start to open!

Of course, you can't outrun your belief system. If there's still a part of you that doesn't truly believe what you desire can and will actually happen, it won't. So if you feel a twinge of doubt, or feel things just aren't coming together as they should, don't let your imagination take you back into old negative habits. Revisit The Soul-Math Formula and do a diagnostic worksheet to reveal your hidden beliefs against manifesting the things you desire. You'll be glad you did.

From Getting to Giving

If you've got a problem on your hands, or find yourself in an unhappy situation, you might consider whether or not you're in a *getting* mode—trying to *get* something from someone or some situation outside yourself. It may be more attention, praise, cooperation, compensation, approval, or simply agreement. It all depends on the problem.

If the problem is with your job, your thoughts may always be on *getting* something from your boss or coworkers. If it's about financial lack, your focus may be on *getting* more money. If it's your kids, you may be focused on *getting* them to do or be whatever you want them to do or be.

To resolve the problem—for everyone's highest good—begin by turning *yourself* around. Look in the other direction. The secret is in the *positive opposite of getting*. In other words, *giving*.

Now I'm not just talking about giving money or other handouts. I'm talking about giving positive self-expression—your talents, understanding, forgiveness, and yourself—as a positive investment in your life. Simply put, I'm talking about bringing your positive attributes and a positive attitude to everything you do.

Notice how whenever you want to *get* something from someone else, you often spend time complaining and demanding they change or do things your way. What generally happens is you waste your time being unproductive, unimaginative, unresponsive, self-pitying, or even angry. The thing is, often the people we blame, judge, or criticize are totally oblivious about it. They just simply go about their merry way. But you— the blamer, judge, and critic—cause yourself to be miserable, ineffective, paralyzed, static, and resentful. And guess what? These are clues. You may have even more forgiving to do!

Enormous amounts of energy can be wasted on accusation, blame, and demands upon others to *get* them to change something. More than likely, nothing will change because they may also have a need to be right. But I've seen many miracles happen when one person stops and does the *positive opposite.* That is, they make a 180-degree turn by beginning to think and feel in positive opposite ways and then initiate a positive opposite action. You see, once you begin to understand instead of disagree, love instead of hate, and offer constructive ideas instead of selfish opinions, things begin to shift. That's when you begin to *give to* a situation instead of try to *take from* it. That's when transformation occurs.

Once you start the ball rolling in a positive opposite direction with sincere and unselfish thoughts, feelings, and actions, you'll find yourself attracting the exact same things from others involved. Resistances and barriers will begin to break down, and resolution may come in a way no one expected because suddenly there's room for creative thinking. But someone must make the first move to get out of their *getting* mode and into a *giving* one.

Giving might take the form of *giving up* something. When you give up complaining, judging, fighting, hating, grudge-holding, criticizing, laziness, and indulging in self-pity, you will experience the freedom to begin positive self-expression. You will be renewed, and your good will keep flowing.

For example, if you're lonely, it's because you're trying to *get* the world to come to you. That's backward. If you want to obliterate loneliness, you must *give*. You must become involved in life. There are endless ways to do this, whether it be to volunteer your time to help others or by participating and interacting with others with the intention of giving. Joining with people of like mind in small discussion groups—not pity-parties—is a valuable and empowering way to share with others, stimulate compassion and bonding, and experience empathy and connection. These are always giving opportunities. Just making a U-turn from a *getting* attitude to a *giving* attitude will heal many of the thoughts and feelings that are causing you unhappiness.

You may ask, "But what about those who are takers and seem to get away with it?" I suggest that those who habitually take from others have lost touch with the seed of a nobler sense of purpose buried deep in their hearts. They have become lost in lower-level thoughts and emotions. The best we can do is honor that within them that is noble, no matter how deeply buried it seems to be and how much we abhor their behavior. That's called true forgiveness! The benefits these people seem to reap are of a superficial and fleeting nature.

Your next questions may be "So what if I do my best to love and honor someone who hurts others and creates difficult situations for them? Won't they just continue to hurt others if they aren't punished? And won't I be condoning their behavior?"

It would be too idealistic to stand back and do nothing in a world where people are continually hurting others. At this point in history, there is still a need for societal laws, jails, a strong police force, an army, and national defense. But there is so much that each of us can do to shine our light into the human world.

Changing the world begins with each individual. We can look beyond physical appearances and choose to see that which is buried beneath the fear. We can choose to honor that which is beyond the crime, hurt, and behavior and at the same time allow the law of cause and effect to operate.

As you conduct yourself in this way, you will find yourself more and more immune to hurt in your own experience. You will find yourself operating at a higher level, on a higher plane of awareness, where you won't even be aware that there are lower-level activities going on around you. I don't mean indulging in denial but operating from a level of awareness that observes the ugliness from a place of detached interest. As more and more of us lift our individual perspectives, there will be major changes in the collective consciousness that could finally transform the outer world. I love how author Ram Dass said it: "The world is perfect as it is, including my desire to change it."

If you're honest with yourself, you will notice that when you're faced with a dilemma involving someone whose behavior you don't like, you're faced with someone who is teaching you a lesson, giving you an opportunity to be an example, or an opportunity to practice true forgiveness.

The Journey from Good to Better to Best!

Where you are on your journey of life may or may not seem particularly good right now. Or maybe certain aspects of it feel good but others don't. Then again, you may be thinking, "Things are good right now, but they sure could be better!" So what if there were something better? And what if "better" could be elevated to what you would describe as the BEST?

Of course, what you consider "good" may be within your comfort zone. You know what I'm talking about. You're feeling okay, your daily routine runs smoothly, and other than being busy, things are … well, *good*. But what about *better*? *Better* is when something outside that comfort zone of yours takes you to something unexpected like more money, a better job, a new relationship, a spiritual aha, an answer to prayer, or perhaps healing. And you might go from *good* to *better* simply by going outside and enjoying nature or heading home to a great dinner and a quiet, relaxed evening after a day of hard work.

So if better sounds pretty good to you, how about *best*? *Best* occurs once all aspects of your consciousness settle into a consistent attitude and perspective that never lets anything in the human world rock your boat. *Best* is fearlessly taking appropriate action and demonstrating your talent, creativity, compassion, gratitude, and the task at hand to the best of your ability in the moment, absolutely *knowing* you have surpassed just feeling comfortable or good. Best is knowing you are *doing* your best, honoring your best self, and knowing that no matter what happens you can wisely and confidently handle it.

This good, better, best idea isn't new. It's routinely applied in the world of product sales. It's called "upselling." Upselling means making the customer aware about the differences in one product or service over another. This way they quickly understand their options and that they get what they pay for. For instance, in advertising, many companies feature perhaps three products of different quality and price ranges. But instead of using the words *good, better,* and *best* to label a product, they'll use words like *economy, standard,* and *premium,* or *bronze, silver,* and *gold,* or even *basic, intermediate,* and *advanced.* The idea, of course, is to give the customers a choice and a basis for comparison, thus increasing their comfort level in making a decision about the investment they make in that product.

So we can see how good, better, and best can be applied not only to things but also to the state of our human condition and our journey in life. We can compare the *price,* or the cost, with respect to emotional charges and material satisfaction between the standard product of life and the premium experience requiring our investment in quality assurance, or our thoughts, feelings, beliefs, and actions.

Now when we look at our *overall* world today and evaluate what's happening from the purely human perspective, things don't even come close to an evaluation of *good* or even *acceptable.* Part of the reason the world appears so chaotic and crazy is because we are privy to so much instant information about what's going on all over the globe, and that information is filtered through the consciousness of those taking the pictures and reporting the news. And as far as the news media is concerned, product sales is all about whether their coverage is good, better, or best when compared to the drama, horror, and emotional stimulation produced by others in the news media arena. The same thing is true of TV programs and movies. From the industry point of view, the more emotional stimulation, shock value, and fear they can generate in their viewers, the better.

The thing is, we all say we want peace, personal peace and world peace. Yet it's the violence and drama that titillates our emotional responses to the point of "awfulizing," "horriblizing," and "catastrophizing," rather than choosing personal peace, expressing gratitude for the good, and using our energy for the highest and *best product of life* within our realm of influence.

When you reach that point where you stop comparing prices between your worth and someone else's, or your level of ability with someone else's, that's when you start moving your experience of life from what feels good to better and eventually to best. It's all about taking responsibility to begin that journey! And you begin that journey by always being your best self and doing your best, even though that can change from moment to moment. The interesting thing is, as you journey from good to better to best, it may not require a change in your *outer* world, simply your inner world.

So what can you do to get your attention focused in the right direction on your journey from good to better to best? First, focus upon gratitude every day, many times a day. That will turn your attention from what you think is missing to the blessings you have that support you.

Second, start giving. How? You can seed money into the world with no strings attached. You can *help* someone with no strings attached. You can *start* something that you've been procrastinating about. You can invest new creative energy into your job, even if it's a job you hate because it's so boring. You can get busy with your résumé if you want your good to get better. You can call someone and ask for what you want. All of these things are matters of adjusting your thoughts, feelings, and beliefs in such a way that there's no hesitation or interference with respect to taking the right *action* that gets things moving.

Finally, you can jump-start your creative thinking. What action can you take that you haven't considered up until now? What impulse has nagged at you over and over, but you haven't listened? What talent have you let go dormant? What can you do today to start giving and expressing yourself in a positive way? This gets your attention off any apparent problem and helps you focus on simply doing your best.

As you're doing your best, you will experience the intensity of life. You will be productive and respectful of yourself, your family, friends, and community—of everything. But it's the *action* that will produce the *best* intensity and increase your happiness.

Remember, being your best and doing your best is all about moving forward and taking action because you love it, not because you're expecting a reward. Of course, if you get a reward for doing your best, that's great! It will be a surprise that leads you from good to better to best. You see, most people go to work every day thinking about the paycheck. They can hardly wait for the end of their shift, the weekend, or just some time off. They're working for the reward, and as a result, they resist doing the work. They want to avoid the action that can lead them from good to better to best. As a result, life becomes more difficult, and of course, they aren't doing their best!

When you find yourself in a pattern of negativity, you have more than likely been wrapping your arms around some big, immovable rock of a problem, and you have pushed, pulled, shoved, sweated, and strained, depleting your energy. Be aware. Notice where you are and get back into action. Climb back up to good where you can open the door of your comfort zone, and make that good better and that better the best!

Be a Solution Person

It's been said there are essentially two kinds of people in the world: those who focus on the problem— analyzing it, complaining about it, revisiting it, and becoming part of it—and those who encounter a challenge and immediately leap over the problem in search of a solution. For the person who becomes enmeshed in the problems of life, life is a struggle. For the person who leaps over the problem and seeks a solution, life is a series of opportunities.

When I say, "Leap over the problem," it might bring all kinds of images to mind—an obstruction blocking your path, a runner leaping over the hurdles, or even a cow jumping over the moon! Whatever the image, it's always about getting over and beyond some obstruction in order to feel freedom, experience healing, fulfill a desire, or find a solution.

The thing is so many people see life as one big problem instead of an adventure to be enjoyed. They see life as one obstacle after another, and it seems as if they'll never get beyond the obstacles. Many of us let the hurdles of life control us. We encounter a problem, and we get stuck in it. Then we struggle through it only to walk into the next challenge, and the next, and the next. Pretty soon, we're programmed with fear, dreading the next bout with difficulty, insecurity, and self-doubt instead of optimism, trust, and enthusiasm about what's next. The result? We keep pushing our good away from us instead of opening to feelings of well-being as we enjoy the solution.

So are you a *problem* person or a *solution* person? Being a solution person is to think and act in ways that improve things in one's mental, emotional, and physical environment. It means taking action within our own realm of influence to alleviate struggle. If war and violence is what we want to help change, we must first act to end it within ourselves. We must learn not to hate or condemn. We must learn to constructively deal with anger when it comes up. But as long as we carry the problem around inside us, we are part of the problem and not the solution. We are stuck in unforgiveness.

Sometimes a solution is right under our noses, but we're problem-focused and don't see it. There's a cute story about a beautiful pedigreed cat that lived in a huge mansion. This cat had everything! It ate out of silver dishes, drank filtered water, and enjoyed all the comforts any cat could want.

The cat's owner liked to sit in front of the fireplace with the cat on his lap, gently petting him. The cat hated it because its owner always petted him against the grain of his fur—he was literally rubbing him the wrong way! One day, the cat had taken all he could take and couldn't stand it anymore, so he ran away.

The pampered cat was in an alley looking for food in a garbage can when an alley cat came up to him and asked, "What are *you* doing in this alley?" The beautiful cat explained that it had to run away because it was being rubbed the wrong way and just couldn't take it anymore.

The alley cat said, "You didn't need to run away! You just had to turn the other way on the pillow!"

The pedigreed cat was so caught up in the problem that the simple solution hadn't even occurred to him. Instead, he ran away. Isn't that what we often do when we become part of the problem? We become so unhappy and frustrated that we can't see any solution other than running away or avoidance.

I can't tell you how many times I've talked with people who have become so immersed in a problem that the only solution they can see is to run away. It takes courage, creativity, and discipline to look for solutions. Now granted, there may come a point where the best solution is to simply walk away from an irreversible problem. But even that can happen with a calm attitude about learning rather than just giving up. Another version of running away or giving up is passing the buck. "Here. You solve this problem." (That way I don't have to risk failure.)

Why is life so hard for *problem* people? Because what they're best at is seeing all kinds of ways something can't be done. They will talk about the problem to anyone who will listen. They feed the problem with their time and energy and have very little left with which to think straight or take positive, caring action. Unforgiveness, here we come!

Why is life easier for *solution* people? Well, things tend to move better because they cooperate with the flow of possibility thinking. They understand the place to start is remembering that the most important basic thing guiding every experience in the human world is *thought*. Everything begins with a thought. What we think about expands. Oh, I know you've heard this a million times, but somebody has to keep reminding us because we so often forget.

There are five major steps to being a solution person. First, be *aware* of the problem but *willing* to seek a solution. This means mentally stepping back, shaking off fear, and looking upon the problem with interest but not dwelling on it or talking about it unless it's absolutely necessary. Size things up while noticing the bigger picture—around and beyond the problem—where you just might spot a perfect solution. In other words, leap over the problem!

Second, get clear about what you want, how you want to feel, and the direction in which you would like to move. Then practice monitoring your thoughts and keeping them focused on a solution, not the problem.

Third, bring yourself to a point where you *believe* that a solution, in the best interest of everyone concerned, is possible.

Fourth, take an action. The first action is to ask, *believing* there's a solution. I'm not talking about asking in a desperate or pleading way, but asking in a way that's partnered with faith that a solution is forthcoming. This asking might be directed toward the God of your understanding or perhaps another person who would be helpful in a positive way. Then do what's before you to do. If something occurs to you more than once, and moving on that idea won't hurt you or anyone else, don't hesitate. Do it!

Taking positive action in the right direction will lead to synchronicities that will most assuredly show up to guide you toward the best solution.

Finally, take time out every day to get quiet by meditating, doing some deep breathing exercises, or taking a walk in nature. Whatever method you choose, use that time to consider all the things you have to be grateful for.

By following these suggestions, you can move beyond the appearance of a problem and into the promise of solution. Then the next time you find yourself being rubbed the wrong way, you can just turn around on your pillow!

You've Got to Do the Work!

The Chinese philosopher, Lao-tzu once said, "The journey of a thousand miles begins with one step." This reminds us, we can't get anywhere unless we start. We can't just sit still and wish, or think that what we want will fall out of the sky into our lap. We all have to get off our "ifs, ands, and buts" and start moving in the direction of our desires or intentions. But we must have the courage to take the first step.

Someone once asked the Greek philosopher Socrates how to get to Mount Olympus. His answer was "Just make sure that every step you take is in *that* direction."

This is good advice. We're all on a journey of sorts. And on this journey we bring with us our dreams, desires, and longings for fulfillment and happiness. But sometimes the effort to start moving toward those dreams and desires seems too great, and we find ourselves overwhelmed and frozen in disappointment, despair, procrastination, or a comfort zone we're afraid to step beyond. And as I mentioned at the very beginning of this book, many of us fail to realize that unforgiveness is the real culprit holding us back and immobilizing us.

The thing is, if you remain frozen and doing nothing, you'll never find your Mount Olympus. You'll never make any progress unless you get started. Why is it so hard to get started? The basic answer is fear. One of the greatest fears is making a decision, especially a decision to start moving toward your desire. I heard about one woman who said, "Sometimes I feel like a donkey standing between two bales of hay, unable to decide which bale of hay I want. In the meantime, I'm starving to death!"

The terrible irony about being afraid to make a decision is that by not deciding or choosing, we are deciding to starve ourselves of that which is important, meaningful, supportive, and fulfilling. But we're afraid that a wrong decision will take something away from us, like money, friendships, security, or status. So many of us are afraid of making mistakes. Especially the perfectionists. We forget that we learn from our mistakes, and our need to be perfect and to control the outcome of everything keeps us anchored in fear when we think about taking the first step toward change. And keep in mind that fear has to come from somewhere, and often it has its roots in unforgiveness.

As you muster up the courage to take that first step, or perhaps the next step, and you encounter fear, think about this: you can never fear a person, thing, or first step unless you've already given power to that person, thing, or fear.

There's no way around it: you've got to do the work. That work includes applying the Forgiveness Process to remove the mental and emotional interferences anchoring you in place. It includes digging into your subconscious with The Soul-Math Formula and discovering the thoughts, feelings, and beliefs you didn't know lurked in the background. It includes doing the consciousness U-turns that can help you get moving in the right direction.

Remember: every journey begins with the first step, and the first step can be the hardest because of what is termed the *law of inertia*. This is a physics principle. The word *inertia* comes from a Latin word meaning idle or lazy. It's the tendency for a mass to resist motion, action, or change. A mass tends to just sit there. Each one of us could be considered a mass, a lump of physical stuff that gets to choose when it's going to move.

The science of physics proves that it actually takes more energy to get a stationary mass moving than it does to keep it moving. For instance, it takes a lot more energy to get a train moving from a still position than it does to keep it moving down the tracks. So if we consider ourselves to be that stationary mass, getting ourselves moving in the direction of our desire is the hardest part of our journey. Once we get moving, we pick up momentum and forward movement is easier. Once we get moving, we generate motivation. Motivation doesn't come first; we turn motivation on inside ourselves once we take that first step.

True forgiveness can be the thing that gets us moving and keeps us going! Don't waste your time thinking you have nothing to forgive! Get busy. Do the work. Then feel the freedom as you move forward with ease, enthusiasm, and joy in your heart.

The simple truth is, your dreams and intentions come true as the result of your active participation. You create your own happiness, peace of mind, joy, fulfillment, and wholeness of body, mind, and spirit by putting the cell phone or remote down once in a while and looking out the window beyond your limited perceptions and noticing the bigger picture. The next step is to follow the bigger picture. To do that, you have to leave the living room. You have to do something different. You have to take the first step. You've got to do the work!

FINAL THOUGHTS

*I can't imagine a person becoming a success who doesn't
give this game of life everything he's got.*
—Walter Cronkite

So there you have it. If you've read this far without skipping any chapters, it's time to undertake the journey of freedom into authentic forgiveness and happiness. The important thing is, don't stop here just because you've finished reading the book!

I wrote this book to give you ways to successfully unplug from the painful memories of unkind, thoughtless, or terrible actions of other people as well as yourself. I wrote this book to help you realize that old emotional wounds that have faded from conscious memory can still be registered in the cells of your body and cause great physical harm if not revealed at a conscious level and forgiven. I wrote this book to help you see that forgiveness is much more complex than just saying, "I forgive." I wrote this book because I want for you the same freedom I have discovered for myself.

From a very practical perspective, when we don't heal into forgiveness, some of our opportunity to experience the highest quality of life is shut down. We become frozen in time, emotionally anchored to some experience, and to the degree we hang onto our anger, resentment, and hate, we lock ourselves away in a prison of pain. We then become unavailable to the higher experiences of happiness, peace, and contentment. We need to remember that the same body/mind/soul mechanism that feels the emotions of unforgiveness is the same system that feels peace and love. And we can't do both at the same time.

I ask of you a couple of things. First, remember, when you work through the Forgiveness Process and completely unplug from just one person or event, it will be easier to slide into authentic forgiveness concerning other such memories. Why? Because many similar past wounds could have glommed onto that same emotional umbilical cord, making it thicker and thicker. As you take the steps to trim the circumference of that cord, it will get thinner and thinner. When it finally unplugs, you may be detaching from a number of things all at once. Just think how freeing that will be!

Second, please remember to start every day with the things essential to your body, mind, and spirit. Because these things are personal to you, only you know exactly what they are. Do them. I would hope they include forgiveness work, prayer, meditation, and exercise. Do these things first and the rest of the day will seem longer and you'll accomplish more than expected.

Finally, remember that true forgiveness is so much more than just releasing another person from blame. It's about releasing yourself and opening the door to magnificent new possibilities.

There's absolutely nothing like the experience of genuine forgiveness! Once you get there, make sure you monitor your thoughts, feelings, beliefs, and actions so you never again plug an emotional umbilical cord into anyone or anything. May you walk the path of peace, lightness, love, strength, courage, and meaning as you move forward in life. YOU DESERVE IT!

Men suffer all their life long,
under the foolish superstition that they can be cheated.
But it is impossible for a man to be cheated
by anyone but himself.
—Ralph Waldo Emerson

ABOUT THE AUTHOR

Phylis Sparks is a professional speaker, teacher, workshop facilitator, seminar leader, and author of *SOUL-ESTEEM: The Power of Spiritual Confidence*. A graduate of Washington University in Saint Louis, Missouri, and the Ernest Holmes College School of Ministry, she currently conducts classes on Effective Speaking and Presentation Skills, Meditation, Prosperity Principles, The Soul-Math Formula, The Technology of Prayer, Mirrors of Relationship, and many others. Phylis was a Dale Carnegie instructor for eight years and a very successful interior designer and artist. She writes many articles on self-development for various publications and is the founder and director of The Soul-Esteem Center in Maryland Heights, Missouri. She lives in Lake Saint Louis, Missouri, with her husband, Bill Lange.

Printed in the United States
By Bookmasters